Giving Up god
. . . To Find God

Giving Up god
. . . To Find God

Breaking Free of Idolatry

KERRY WALTERS

ORBIS BOOKS
Maryknoll, New York 10545

Founded in 1970, Orbis Books endeavors to publish works that enlighten the mind, nourish the spirit, and challenge the conscience. The publishing arm of the Maryknoll Fathers and Brothers, Orbis seeks to explore the global dimensions of the Christian faith and mission, to invite dialogue with diverse cultures and religious traditions, and to serve the cause of reconciliation and peace. The books published reflect the views of their authors and do not represent the official position of the Maryknoll Society. To learn more about Maryknoll and Orbis Books, please visit our website at www.maryknollsociety.org.

Library of Congress Cataloging-in-Publication Data

Walters, Kerry S.
  Giving up god...to find God / Kerry Walters.
       pages cm
    Includes bibliographical references.
    ISBN 978–1–62698–042–6 (pbk.)
    1. Spirituality—Catholic Church. 2. Idolatry. 3. Idols and images—
Worship. I. Title.
    BX2350.65.W346 2013
    248.4—dc23

                                                    201300148

For Karl Mattson,
breaker of idols

And as always,
for Kim and Jonah

*Every man becomes the image of the God
he adores.
He whose worship is directed to a dead
thing
becomes a dead thing.
He who loves corruption rots.
He who loves a shadow becomes, himself, a
shadow.
He who loves things that must perish
lives in dread of their perishing.
The man who leaves the Lord the freedom
of the Lord
adores the Lord in His freedom and receives
the liberty of the sons of God.*

—THOMAS MERTON
NO MAN IS AN ISLAND

Contents

Preface

You act like mortals in all that you fear, and like immortals in all that you desire.

—SENECA

Man is indeed out of his mind. He cannot even create a flesh-worm, yet creates gods by the dozen.

—MICHEL DE MONTAIGNE[1]

This is a book about idolatry, both the disease—for a spiritual disease it surely is—and its treatment.

Whenever we succumb to idolatry, or the worship of false gods, we fall victim to a kind of spiritual insanity that puts a brand-new twist on the old Greek maxim that the gods first make mad whom they would destroy. In the case of idolatry, our own madness creates the gods who wind up destroying us. Idolaters are indeed, in the brutal but accurate words of the sixteenth-century essayist Montaigne, out of their minds. For what person in full possession of his or her faculties would prefer artifact to reality, especially when the reality that's forsaken is the living God?

---

[1] Seneca, "On the Shortness of Life," in *Dialogues and Letters*, ed. C. D. N. Costa (New York: Penguin, 1997), 60; Michel de Montaigne, "An Apology for Raymond Sebond," in *Complete Essays*, trans. M. A. Screech (New York: Penguin, 1993), 594.

And yet we make that choice all the time. Driven by puling anxieties and inflated lusts—Seneca hit the nail on the head when he said that we humans fear like mortals but desire like gods—we clutch at false deities who can, we tell ourselves, give us everything we want without requiring anything from us in return. But like all delusions, idolatrous ones can't endure for long. Even if the idols we tailor bestow a false sense of security in the short run, they betray us sooner or later. Then the very gods we hoped would protect and serve us become demons who drag us ever further away from what our hearts *really* desire but our timidity forgets: a relationship with the sometimes elusive, always mysterious, utterly unmanageable, and forever transformative presence of God.

As with all maladies, the first step in overcoming idolatry is learning to recognize both its causes and symptoms. So in Chapter 1 I provide a clinical etiology that traces idol worship back to its root causes. Although much more ancient than the Hebraic golden calf, idolatry is a cunning disease that easily accommodates itself to the historical and cultural specifics of each generation. Chapters 2 through 11 offer diagnostic descriptions of the ten most common ways idolatry afflicts us today. Although I suggest therapeutic tips along the way for coping with these various forms of idolatry, my full prescription is reserved for the concluding Chapter 12.

Like many physical illnesses—malaria, for example, or the flu—the spiritual malady of idolatry can be recurrent. Some people are so chronically afflicted by it that it becomes a more or less permanent debilitation. But for most of us idolatrous temptations tend to come and go. Periods of special stress can bring on attacks; curiously, so can periods of spiritual dullness or complacency. The environment in which we live almost always influences the frequency with which we will succumb to idolatry. One of my claims in this book is that contemporary American culture is an especially fertile medium for the growth of idolatries.

As you read this book, you may recognize a particular form of idolatry that you recall suffering from in the past or perhaps feel yourself slipping into now. You may even have firsthand familiarity with more than one of the various kinds of idolatry I describe. In fact, I'd be surprised if things were otherwise. Different idolatries attack us at different stages of our spiritual development. Looking at my own life, for example, I'm pretty sure that I've fallen into a good one-third of the idolatries I discuss in this book. It doesn't help that many of them cluster with one another, so that an embrace of one ensures that several others tag along for the ride. Most idolatry is a form of polytheism.

Also like many other maladies, idolatry typically doesn't get cured once and for all. The Psalmist reminds us that we humans are like grass that dies in a day and is thrown on the fire. It's foolish of us to deny our frailty. It's an inescapable fact about who we are, even if we try to pretend otherwise. The deep-seated anxiety it brews within us periodically boils over in dreadful moments of panic or despair, which in turn make us particularly susceptible to the contagion of idolatry. We will experience these dark nights of the soul all our lives, and so we will never escape the temptation to scurry in desperation to idols that offer us false hopes of protection.

When it comes to treating idolatry, then, the goal isn't to make it vanish—that's too unrealistic to take seriously—so much as to control and contain it. The key, as we'll discover, is recognition that our essential frailty as humans, although always frightening, is also a blessing, because it can lead us to a grateful and awe-filled awareness of our dependency on God's grace. God is the supreme Physician who ceaselessly offers therapy—God's very self—for our susceptibility to idolatry. The more we direct our attention to God, the better able we are to give up the false gods birthed by our inordinate anxieties and desires. Given the human condition, there may be no final cure for idolatry this side of the grave. But the divine Healer is always available to move us through the latest crisis and closer to the health he intends for us.

Chapter 1

Why we need
to give up god

> *Daily experience teaches that the flesh is always uneasy until it has obtained some figment like itself in which it may fondly find solace as in an image of God.*
>
> —JOHN CALVIN

> *I am the cause of God's existence as god.*
>
> —MEISTER ECKHART[1]

Whenever the thirteenth-century theologian Meister Eckhart preached, much of what he said went over the heads of the good people of Strasbourg, the city where he lived. Straining to follow his sometimes brain-cracking subtleties, they often latched onto any isolated phrase along the way that seemed to

---

[1] Chapter epigraphs are from John Calvin, *Institutes of the Christian Religion* (Peabody, MA: Hendrickson, 2008), 55; and Meister Eckhart, *Selected Writings,* trans. Oliver Davies (New York: Penguin, 1994), 208.

make sense. But because the lines were ripped out of context, they were usually misunderstood. So, shocked at what they *thought* he'd said, upset congregants regularly complained to the bishop. Eckhart was always in trouble of one sort or another with the church hierarchy.

A sound bite wrenched from one sermon in particular landed Eckhart in especially hot water. He was preaching on the first beatitude, "Blessed are the poor in spirit," when he said something that knocked the wind out of his audience. It still packs a wallop today. We ought, Eckhart said, "to pray God to rid us of God."[2] What was Eckhart getting at? Surely not, as his scandalized congregants assumed, that we should throw God over. Eckhart was an intensely religious man. There's no way that his sermon was either a declaration of disbelief or an attempt to subvert the faith. Instead, what he wanted to do was to exhort his listeners to think about whether the God they worshiped was in fact the *true* God or one of their own making. He wasn't advising them, or us, to get rid of God, but rather of the idols we mistake for God.

Eckhart's meaning becomes clearer if we simply shift one letter down from an upper to a lower case: We pray *God* to rid us of *god*. If that doesn't get the job done, the phrase that came next in his sermon—one that got overshadowed by all the uproar—does: ". . . so that we may grasp and eternally enjoy the truth." We should, with God's help, get rid of our idols in order to dispel illusion and connect with reality. Worshiping false gods draws us deeper and deeper into the darkness of falsehood and further away from the living God of truth. If we pray to God for anything, it should be deliverance from that.

Eckhart's sermon was deeply subversive, although not in the way that some of his listeners thought, because in it he sought to draw attention to and undermine the effortlessness with which we humans can substitute what we *want* God to

[2] Meister Eckhart, Sermon 52, in Oliver Davies, trans., *Selected Writings* (New York: Penguin, 1994), 205.

be for who God actually *is*. We create our golden calves and fall down before them, unaware—in part because we don't want to admit to ourselves what we're up to—that the deity we worship, although perhaps offering us some kind of short-term dividend, doesn't have the juice to enable us to "grasp and eternally enjoy the truth." Even worse, the idols we think will give us what we want inevitably wind up hoodwinking us. They take without giving much of anything in return. The worship of them is an addiction that, regardless of how good it feels in the beginning, insidiously saps our spiritual health and enslaves our souls.

Iron gods and fear

Pierre Teilhard de Chardin, the twentieth-century scientist, theologian, and mystic, once confessed that he'd fallen into idolatry as a young boy. He collected scraps of metal such as shell casings and broken bits of plow and reverently placed them on a makeshift altar in his bedroom. "You should have seen me," he wrote, "as in profound secrecy and silence I withdrew into the contemplation of my 'God of Iron.' A God, note, of iron; and why iron? Because in all my childish experience there was nothing in the world harder, tougher, more durable than this wonderful substance." But the inevitable day came when his iron god failed him: "I can never forget the pathetic depths of a child's despair when I realized one day that iron can be scratched and can rust. I had to look elsewhere for substitutes that would console me."[3]

We mustn't dismiss Teilhard's iron god as a childish bit of pretending. What attracted him to it was its seeming indestructibility. If something this strong existed, the boy reasoned, perhaps he could curry its favor and gain for himself some protection from the frightening world. In paying

---

[3] Pierre Teilhard de Chardin, *The Divine Milieu* (New York: Harper and Row, 1968), 18.

obeisance to the iron god, Teilhard hoped to find a remedy for fear.

This is precisely the logic of idolatry. What makes a notion of God idolatrous is its being born of fear. Everyone occasionally turns to God out of a sense of anxiety or fright. We all experience crises in our lives that overwhelm us, and during such times it's perfectly natural to seek divine comfort and solicit divine aid. But fear ought not be our primary motive for turning to God in the first place; neither ought we to worship God mainly to coax God into protecting us from all the things that frighten us. This kind of deity very quickly becomes little more than a stand-in for everything we want out of life, an idol fashioned not out of iron so much as fears, anxieties, needs, and demands. Nineteenth-century atheist Ludwig Feuerbach argued that the Divine is nothing more than a projection of human qualities we admire: wisdom, love, compassion, and so on.[4] But for idolaters, it's not really essential that their god be wise or loving or compassionate, although it's nice if he is. All they truly require is that their deity be powerful enough to absorb all of the fears and insecurities they feel inadequate to handle and to give them what they want but feel unable to obtain on their own. They want a god that demands nothing and gives everything.

Stories about idolatry in the Bible all fit this mold. Just consider two of the best known. Wandering in the desert, the Hebrew people fall down before the golden calf because they've come to distrust the God of Moses. They fear the wilderness and long for the days when they were in bondage to Pharaoh. At least then they weren't lost and frightened. Their hope is that paying homage to this new god will fix the situation in which they find themselves. The New Testament tells us that in another desert several centuries later, Jesus confronts and successfully resists the temptations that assail

---

[4] Feuerbach makes his case in his 1841 *Das Wesen des Chrsitentums*. The book was translated from German into English by novelist George Eliot and titled *The Essence of Christianity* (1854).

every human being: lust for material possessions, for power, and for acclaim. Satan says to him, Worship me and all your anxieties about destitution, impotence, and anonymity will be fixed! But the real temptation in the story, the one that generates the other three, is idolatry, worship of the false god Satan. Jesus, unlike the Hebrews in the wilderness, managed to overcome the fear that breeds idolatry. Yet both stories attest to the fact that it's a constant temptation. Angelic messengers throughout the Bible cry out, "Do not fear!" for good reason. Their proclamation is partly reassurance, but also warning. It's not only pride that comes before a downfall. So does fear.

None of this should be much of a surprise. We know from personal experience as well as cultural memory that fear can drive us to give our allegiance to whomever and whatever we believe can protect us. Sick patients often cling desperately to an unrealistic confidence in their physicians' ability to heal them, desperate masses blindly follow charismatic political leaders, and true believers of all stripes clutch at their various "isms" with steely grips. We also know that fear is a powerful religious motivator. As the old saying goes, there are no atheists in foxholes. (There actually are, as it turns out, but you get the point.)

Speaking of atheists, some of them are better than believers at spotting the connection between fear and religion. Sigmund Freud, for one, recognized that much of what passes for religion is really idolatry because it focuses on ameliorating the fear that haunts humans. According to Freud, we go through life quaking from three primal threats to our well-being. We fear an unpredictable natural world that can strike us down at any moment with earthquake, blizzard, drought, or lowly microbe; we fear our fellow humans, whom we see as merciless competitors for the goods we desire; and most of all, we fear death. In order to cope with these terrors, we invent—unknowingly, of course—a divine parent who will protect us just as our earthly parents did when we were youngsters. We ascribe to this god-parent the power to fix the things that frighten us by controlling the material world, reining in the wickedness of others (or at least punishing them if they *do* wind up harming us), and giving us an afterlife. We offer this god our allegiance in return for him keeping us safe. Religion, in other words, becomes a protection racket.[5]

You don't have to be an atheist to agree with Freud that there's something fishy about fear-motivated religion. The twentieth-century Christian martyr Dietrich Bonhoeffer likewise sensed that a religion based upon fear is more idolatrous than authentic. His special worry was that Christianity, which properly ought to be a religion of joy and gratitude, was increasingly one whose adherents turn to God only when they're in distress. God, he feared, had become a *deus ex machina* trotted out "either for the apparent solution of insoluble problems, or as strength in human failure."[6] Bonfoeffer's use of language here is revealing. A *deus ex machina*, literally "god out of the machine," was a stage device whose origins stretch back to ancient Greek drama and comedy. An actor portraying a god would be lowered by a crane onto the stage to save the day by killing off villains or miraculously thwarting their evil plans. The device was a shortcut that allowed lazy playwrights to avoid the hard work of crafting their plots thoughtfully. It was all very arbitrary, usually quite implausible, and always artistically clumsy.

In worrying that the Christian God is becoming a *deus ex machina,* Bonhoeffer's point was that Christians tend to call on God only when they want a bad situation fixed quickly, neatly, and magically—or, to go back to Freud, when they're frightened enough to appeal to a god-parent. Diagnosed with a life-threatening illness? In danger of bankruptcy or public disgrace? Sunk in the depths of an existential crisis that saps life of meaning? Brokenhearted? These are what Bonhoeffer called

---

[5] Freud makes this argument in several places, but the locus classicus is his 1927 *The Future of an Illusion*. The title's "illusion" is religion, which Freud believes has no "future" now that science is progressively explaining reality.

[6] Dietrich Bonhoeffer, *Letters and Papers from Prison* (New York: Macmillan, 1971), 285.

"boundary" situations, ones that hurl us away from the comfortable center of a stable life into murky regions of uncertainty that paralyze us with fear. But if boundary situations are the only things that prompt us to turn to God, we're in search of a *deus ex machina*. This makes us idolaters, because God isn't a magical talisman who solves all our problems and soothes all our fears, a rabbit's foot that we can shove back in our pockets until the next crisis comes along. Things just aren't that easy.

Interestingly, both Freud and Bonhoeffer arrived at the same conclusion, though by quite different routes. Both suspected that the time had come to consider jettisoning "religion." If, said Freud, it's nothing more than an anxious clinging to the fantasy that a god-parent will step up when we're in trouble, a much more efficient way of alleviating our fears is turning to science. As our scientific knowledge of the universe and its natural laws enlarge our ability to do something about natural disasters, social unrest, and even mortality, religion will die on the vine.

For his part, Bonhoeffer concluded that what might be needed to overcome the mutation of God into a *deus ex machina* is a "religionless Christianity" that weans us from our frightened addiction to a superhero-god whose only task is to pull our chestnuts out of the fire. A Christianity liberated from the fear that breeds idolatry had, Bonhoeffer believed, a chance of re-centering God in our midst rather than exiling him to the hinterlands. To paraphrase Eckhart, it could get rid of god for the sake of God.

What Bonhoeffer—not to mention Freud—didn't take into account is that the idolatrous mutation of God into an idol that fixes whatever frightens or causes us anxiety is an act of deep, deep violence. The contemplative monk Thomas Merton, among others, knew all too well that violence is born of fear.[7] Frightened people see everything as a threat. They dwell

---

[7] A good source for Merton's thoughts on nonviolence is *The Nonviolent Alternative*, a collection of his essays, ed. Gordon Zahn (New York: Farrar, Straus, and Giroux, 1981).

in a hostile universe that they're unable to trust, much less love. So their habitual response to the world is one of fight or flight, and this is the idolaters' modus operandi as well. But in reducing God to god, they not only do themselves no service, but they also act aggressively against God by rejecting the nature with which God has gifted them. They both flee from the living God and fight against their God-given nature as free creatures. Let's see how.

Fleeing freedom

God may be ever present, but unlike iron gods, God is also elusive. Personal experience, the limitations of language, and scriptural authority all testify to this truth. So fidelity to God, as opposed to an idol, can stretch us way beyond our comfort zones. But it also sets us free. Idolatrous worship of more tangible gods, although much less challenging, enslaves us. There's a sad irony here, because the primary goal of idolaters is to find liberation from the fears that inhibit or even paralyze them. But by fearfully latching onto an idolatrous *deus ex machina*, they close off so many possibilities that they wind up snapping on a different set of shackles. What they fail to realize is that in the spiritual arena, just as in the political one, there are two kinds of freedom: freedom-*from* and freedom-*to*. Both are essential for well-being. Giving up one for the sake of the other is a bad deal.

To thrive politically and socially we require a certain amount of freedom from illegitimate interference in our lives. My flourishing depends, for example, on my freedom from grinding poverty or dehumanizing prejudice. In a political context, what constitutes genuine freedom-from may get fuzzy at times—Do I have a right to be free from having to listen to foul language in the subway? Am I entitled to be free from in-your-face advertising gimmicks?—but the principle itself is well established. My well-being depends in part on my not being hog-tied by unnecessary constraints on my freedom.

But my flourishing depends on more than just freedom *from* undue restrictions. It also depends on my freedom *to* explore new possibilities, pursue adventurous courses of action, and entertain beliefs, howsoever unconventional, that may enrich my life. The presumption is that it's not enough to be protected *from* interference or harm. I must also be free *to* creatively pursue fresh opportunities. Freedom-from is all about protection and security, but by itself doesn't necessarily encourage growth. Freedom-to does, although it also brings with it the possibility of failure or danger since it means pushing off into uncharted waters. If I fearfully cling to freedom-from at the expense of freedom-to, I soon find myself in a small room with too little oxygen.

Spiritual flourishing, like social well-being, requires both kinds of freedom. When confronted by boundary crises such as a serious illness or a loved one's betrayal, we need to know that God is our safety net. It's not inappropriate to want God to protect us from evils that may befall us or to salvage us when they strike. The whole practice of intercessory and petitionary prayer is based on the perfectly legitimate conviction that God is our bulwark in times of trouble.

But if our understanding of God as a guarantor of freedom-from is to be spiritually healthy, it must be complemented by confidence that God's profligate love also offers an abundance of freedom-to opportunities. God has thrown open the entire universe for our admiring inspection, and we're free to venture into it as deeply as we dare. We're not made to hunker down inside a safe but static freedom-from bomb shelter. This would be a horrible misuse of freedom. Instead, we're called to be as daring in our spiritual lives as God was in creating us. In accepting our spiritual freedom-to, we forsake safe zones that might make us feel secure but that, if never left, become dead zones. Venturing beyond them will always involve a certain amount of risk—again, just as God took a big chance in creating us in the first place—and this, in turn, will provoke anxiety. But exercising our freedom-to is a necessary condition for rich and deep encounters with the living God, not to mention our fellow humans.

Idolaters don't get this. They forsake freedom-to for the sake of freedom-from. Hounded by their fears, they fancy that they'll finally get shed of them only if they throw in their lot with an iron god who can offer them the ultimate security they crave. What they don't understand is that this sort of arrangement creates an unhealthy relationship based more on need than love, desperation than joy, and demand than request. It breeds a dependency that shies away from the freedom-to risk of spiritual stretching. It infantilizes rather than matures the worshiper. The God of Abraham and Sarah, the God of Jesus and the apostles, simply refuses to offer a bum deal like this.

Another way of putting this is that idolaters miss the difference between clinging and cleaving. They cling to their idol out of desperation and fear, grabbing on to it as a lifeline, obsessively refusing to let it go lest harm befall them. Their god is a fetish that they hope will protect them as long as they clutch it with all their might. Their clinging is purely external, like kudzu wrapping itself around a tree. Their fear inhibits them from letting go long enough to open themselves to God. Doing so would make them too vulnerable. So they perform external oblations and rituals or mumble magical-*cum*-religious incantations, but they never go much deeper than that. During interludes of relative calm, their grip on their idol may loosen just a bit, but rarely enough to allow them to stretch their fingers out full length. The prospect of a Sistine Chapel–like reaching across empty space to touch God's finger terrifies them. And in boundary crises, in the maelstrom of Bonhoeffer's "insoluble problems," the fingers anxiously clutch at the idol.

But cleaving to God is something quite different from clinging to an idol. It's not a product of desperate need or out-of-control fear. Instead, cleaving is a loyalty based on love and trust—both of which are genuine interior movements—that celebrates the freedom-to opportunities bestowed by God while gratefully acknowledging the freedom-from safety net offered by God. Fourteenth-century mystic Dame Julian of Norwich wonderfully expressed this sort of relationship with God in her famous words, "All shall be well, and all shall be well, and all manner of thing shall be well."[8] She knew that adversities and challenges are part of the human condition and that reaching out to the living God can be risky business. But she also knew that the person who truly trusts that God will make "all manner of thing to be well" can face the unknown as a land ripe for spiritual discovery. In this case freedom-from complements rather than stifles freedom-to.

Shrunken gods

So idolatry's first irony—and *irony* is really too tame a word; *tragedy* is more like it—is that in frantically seeking freedom from fear, idolaters shut themselves off from the promise of a more genuine liberation. The second irony is this: the idols to which they turn can't protect them anyway. So in worshiping them, idolaters sell their freedom and get nothing in return except the illusion of safety. It's a horrible trade-off.

The Hebrew prophets memorably scoffed at idolaters for worshiping mere pieces of wood or clay. They thought it absurd that any right-thinking person could be foolish enough to imagine that a carved statue is worthy of devotion. But the lunacy of idolatry goes even further, for idolaters' gods aren't really stone or cypress. They are the idolaters themselves; idolaters are self-worshipers. *They* are the god they worship.

Remember Ludwig Feuerbach's claim that God is nothing more than a projection of commendable human traits?

---

[8] Dame Julian's "All manner of thing shall be well" is in *The Revelation of Divine Love in Sixteen Showings,* which she wrote toward the end of the fourteenth century. The "showings" were revelations from God she'd experienced twenty years earlier during a nearly fatal illness. T. S. Eliot repeated Julian's saying in his "Little Gidding," the fourth of his *Four Quartets.*

Although there's no compelling reason to accept his conclusion that God doesn't exist (of *course* much of what we
believe about God is projection, but this alone isn't enough
to lead to the conclusion that God is nothing *but* projection),
his line of reasoning is insightful when it comes to thinking
about idolatry. An idol is a compensatory reflection of its
worshipers' personal and temperamental fears. To cope, they
longingly imagine an ideal self liberated from them, and this
image serves as the template for the deity whose powers they
invoke. So, the idolater's god is a disguised self-image stripped
of weakness and endowed with the strength for which the
idolater yearns. Idolatrous gods are just ourselves, dressed up
in superhero costumes.

Theologian Paul Tillich cautioned that God and God alone
is our proper ultimate concern.[9] But when we become idolaters, we take our own needs as our ultimate concern. Nothing
is more important, nothing more pressing—nothing more
real—than our need to be free from fear and anxiety. So it's
not surprising that the gods we fashion are made out of our
own idealized self. A timid idolater's god might be an intrepid
warrior self; a sexually repressed idolater's god a dashing
lothario self; a person who thinks she's ugly may wind up
worshiping a god that personifies the beauty she wants for
herself. Our gods are projections of who we want to be.

Put so starkly, it seems incredible that we could fall into
the self-deception of allowing our own insecurities to stage
manage our ultimate concerns. But it happens all the time.
Hypochondriacs and neurotics are obvious examples of anxious self-absorption run amok. Anyone who's ever worked in
a hospital or convalescence facility knows how easy it is for
the pain and suffering of illness to rivet a patient's attention
exclusively and desperately on his or her own comfort. Money
worries, as has been demonstrated time and again since the
financial crisis of 2008, can also lead to self-absorbed panic in

---

[9] For more on Tillich's ultimate concern, consult his *Dynamics of
Faith* (New York: Harper and Row, 1957).

which financial security becomes an ultimate concern. Judging from these and other "boundary situations," it's clear that the *deus ex machina* that idolaters turn to is wrought from the raw material of their fears. Under their psyche's carving knife, the fear is transformed into an ideal self-god powerful enough to battle whatever demons—ill health, death fear, bankruptcy, and so on—the idolaters dread.

The obvious problem with self-worship is that we simply aren't made to be gods. The sum total of all our genuinely praiseworthy qualities doesn't add up to even a demi-god, much less a full-fledged god. How much more inadequate, then, is a god fashioned out of our suppressed insecurities and weaknesses. This kind of god is too small, too shrunken, to give us what we want, much less what we really need. The spirit behind the old legal adage that a defendant who represents himself has a fool for a client applies equally well here. Those who take themselves—even their idealized self— as their god have hitched their wagon to a lousy ultimate concern.

Abracadabra

There's a third tragic irony to idolatry: idolaters think they are in control of the gods they worship. That's one of the reasons they derive such comfort from them. They believe their gods have the power to protect them from whatever it is they fear. But they also believe they know how to manipulate their gods to get what they want. They know the secret name of god that, when invoked, works the magic.

Magic is the appropriate word here, too, because idolaters really *do* think that they can control their gods by properly reciting certain incantations or performing certain rituals. There's a compulsive quality to idolatry: evil can be held at bay by furiously rattling off rosary beads, lighting candles, scrupulously observing novenas, reciting the daily office, spitting over one's shoulder three times, carrying a rabbit's foot, wearing a scapular, and so on. The possibilities are endless. Obviously it's not that prayer and worship are bogus superstitions. Rather, the mechanical and self-serving way in which the idolater performs them transforms vehicles for spiritual discovery and growth into a campaign to control events. For the idolater, reciting the Our Father functions in the same way as waving a magic wand and shouting "Abracadabra!" It's all about forcing god's hand.

But it should be obvious by now that this is all self-deception. As Joy Davidman expressed it, "The essence of idolatry is its attempt to control and enslave the deity. If the idol has power over man, so has man power over the idol; he can bribe it, he can drive a bargain with it, by certain rituals and sacrifices he can compel it to grant his wishes. Or, so, at least, the idolater thinks."[10] Because the gods we substitute for God are compensatory self-projections, they don't serve us so much as keep us locked within the confines of our own insecurities and fears. They absolve us for our lack of courage while at the same time reinforcing thought patterns and behavioral routines that feed the very demons we're trying to escape. Whenever we think we control the gods we worship, we seal ourselves tighter inside an ultimately destructive illusion. The more often we return to them for comfort, the more comfort we need. Obsession becomes addiction. At the end of the day, we are sorcerers' apprentices, unleashing forces we simply can't control. Meister Eckhart knew this.

An idolatrous pantheon

So we turn God into god whenever we allow fear to overwhelm us. God is one, but the idolatrous gods carved from our anxieties are many. Because there's such a variety of idols to choose from, idolaters are often polytheists, worshiping

---

[10] Joy Davidman, *Smoke on the Mountain: An Interpretation of the Ten Commandments.* (Philadelphia, PA: Westminster Press, 1954), 33. Davidman, a gifted poet, was the wife of C. S. Lewis.

more than one god in order to cover as many bases as possible.

In the chapters that follow I offer a pantheon of ten of the most commonly invoked idols today. In their order of appearance they are *Genie god,* who grants wishes (and not just three of them); *Big Brother god,* whose special gift to his devotees is self-righteousness; *Patriot god,* who marches in Fourth of July parades; *We Can Do It! god,* who wants to reform the world; *By the Book god,* who wears the Bible as a sandwich board; *My God,* who cares first for me, and only then (if at all) for you; *Church god,* whom worshipers conflate with ecclesial buildings, canons, and hierarchies; *Designer god,* who follows the latest fashion; *Sunday School god,* who, like Peter Pan, neither grows up nor expects us to; and *Egghead god,* who remains safely—and manageably—abstract.

Of course, merely identifying different idols, while helpful, isn't enough. Recognizing them for what they are doesn't by itself do much to address the fear that turns us to them in the first place. So in the final chapter I'll offer some thoughts, once more invoking wise Meister Eckhart, about how to live with our fear well enough to reach the point of praying God to rid us of gods. Because we are made for freedom, and because a certain level of risk always accompanies freedom, we will never be without some anxiety. But it needn't overwhelm our capacity for love and trust and certainly needn't drive us into the temple-tomb of idolatry.

A final word before we begin exploring our idolatrous pantheon. All of us, at one time or another and to one degree or other, fall into idol worship. No one escapes the anxiety that accompanies the gift of freedom. Each person copes as best he or she can with it. Human frailty being what it is, idolatrous projection is always a possibility. I suspect that even those who do their best to forsake gods for the living God still genuflect before idolatrous altars in moments of weakness, especially in boundary situations. I know I do. So my guess is that very few of us have reason to feel superior to the idolater, because our hearts, at least occasionally, long

for the descent of a *deus ex machina* to save the day. Fortunately, those same hearts are restless until we encounter the
living God, who doesn't promise to make our fears magically
disappear but, much better, *does* promise us genuine freedom.

Chapter 2

Genie god

God wants us to prosper financially, to have plenty of money, to fulfill the destiny he has laid out for us.

—Evangelist Joel Osteen

Modern man, if he dared to be articulate about his concept of heaven, would describe a vision which would look like the biggest department store in the world, showing new things and gadgets, and himself having plenty of money with which to buy them. He would wander around open-mouthed in this heaven of gadgets and commodities.

—Erich Fromm[1]

An acquaintance of mine once told me that she remembered the exact instant she stopped believing in God. It happened

---

[1] Joel Osteen, letter to congregation [Lakewood Church, Houston, TX] (2005); Erich Fromm, *The Sane Society* (New York: Henry Holt, 1955), 135.

when she was eleven years old. She was climbing a tree, lost her footing, and fell to the ground. As soon as she hit, she felt one of her wrists snap. She lay on the ground, clasping the fractured wrist in her good hand and fervently praying for God to heal it. Pretty predictably, nothing happened, "proving" to her that God didn't exist. "That was thirty years ago," she told me, "and I've never since doubted that I was right."

One way of responding to deconversion stories like this is to point out that mature believers don't think of God as an instant miracleworker, and so the absence of immediate responses to prayer isn't a deal breaker when it comes to their faith. But most of us would probably be lying if we denied that there's a little eleven-year-old somewhere inside us who still expects God to give us whatever we ask for and who feels neglected, hurt, and even angry when God doesn't. Why wouldn't we? After all, Jesus assures us that not a sparrow falls from the tree but what the God of love knows about it. These and other sayings of his quite properly lead us to conclude that God also knows when each and every one of us is in trouble. Because God loves us and is all powerful, we go on to conclude that God will come to our rescue, ignoring the inconvenient fact that Jesus never actually says that God *catches* every sparrow that falls.

Moreover, no less an authority than Jesus himself urges us to petition God on our own and others' behalf—"give us today our daily bread." Granted, it may sometimes, and perhaps often, be the case that when we ask God for something, the response is silence. But this doesn't mean that the act of petitioning is foolish. It may just be that the specific boon we ask for is either impossible or not really in our best interests. Or at least so we tell ourselves to make what seems like a rebuff an easier pill to swallow.

So it's hard to condemn the practice of asking God for things. Teresa of Avila, a full-fledged doctor of the church, said that the greater the request we make of God, the more we honor him. Part of her motive, I suspect, was to caution against cluttering God's "in-box" with trivial petitions like "Help me find a parking space!" It can happen that the practice of requesting things of God becomes so thoughtlessly self-centered that it incrementally and insidiously changes the way we think about God. We begin to feel a sense of entitlement, coming to believe that whatever we request, whether healing from stage-four cancer or a winning lottery ticket, is automatically owed us. When this happens, we've transitioned from worshiping God to worshiping Genie god, the god in the magic lamp who, unlike Aladdin's genie, grants us not a measly three wishes but as many as we want—or at least he will once we master the art of coaxing him out of his lamp. Given the sorts of creatures we are, no form of idolatry is more seductive or widespread than this one. Genie god takes pride of place in the idolatrous pantheon.

The gimme habit

If fear breeds idolatry, what's the fear motivating Genie-god devotees? It comes in two flavors. The more peppery one is the prospect of loss: the loss of health, reputation, possessions, loved ones, opportunities, and so on. Everyone reading this has experienced such crises. When they come, we feel as if we're teetering helplessly on the edge of a cliff. All we can do is breathlessly implore. *"Pleasegodpleasegodpleasegod . . . !"* The intensity of these kinds of experiences lodges them in our memories. They become the gold standard when we think about fear.

But there's actually a second flavor of fear that may not normally be as intense but is much more pervasive. It's the fear of not getting something we want. It often flies under the radar because we're usually so fixated on pursuing our desires that we don't notice the background fear of unfulfillment or frustrated appetite that fuels them. But it's there all the same. Whenever we intensely long for something we don't have, we do so not simply because we think it will please us, but also because we anxiously sense, even if only subconsciously, that its lack will bring us discomfort or even distress. Since such a lack upsets our equilibrium, we naturally fear it befalling us.

It's old news that we live in a "gimme" consumer culture that socially and psychologically programs us to want more and more commodities, whether they come as material objects, services, entertainment, or as power and celebrity. Many of our houses might as well be toy chests stuffed to the brim with things bought on impulse and then stashed away once their novelty wears off. The billion-dollar marketing industry knows what it's doing when it comes to seducing us into thinking that we simply *must* have the latest model car, the newest cutting-edge computer gizmo, or the most recent generation Barbie doll. It's also habituated us to thinking of shopping as therapy. If we're depressed, or angry, or even just a bit out of sorts, a trip to the mall or to a favorite cyber store will pick us up in a jiffy, even if our high gets killed when the credit-card bills arrive at the end of the month. Pulitzer Prize–winning cartoonist David Horsey captures this strangely self-destructive form of therapy in a drawing entitled "Reality." As a wife stares despairingly at a stack of bills, saying, "We're going to have to cut back on something," her husband, phone in hand, exuberantly shouts, "No *way!* I just got offered another pre-approved credit card!"

A quick glance at a few statistics indicates just how far sunk we are in the gimme ethos. We Americans spend nearly $6 trillion a year on consumer goods. We spend more on shoes and jewelry than on higher education, and a good chunk of that money gets blown in shopping malls—which, by the way, there are twice as many of as high schools. Seventy percent of us visit a mall each week, way more than attend churches or temples or mosques. If that isn't scary enough, try this one on for size: 93 percent of teenage American girls say that shopping is their favorite activity.

The problem, of course, is that our desires to not lose what we have and to acquire more and more, as well as our underlying anxieties about not satisfying our desires, become so intensely all-consuming (pun intended, by the way) that we begin to mistake them for needs. What were luxuries to an earlier generation strike us today as necessities we absolutely can't live without. We feel we're entitled to them, because life is miserable in their absence and all of us deserve a happy life—right? As our gimme habit grows, so does our expectation that our desires, now transformed by us into needs, will be gratified. When they're not, our underlying anxiety over not getting what we want bubbles to the surface. We feel sorry for ourselves, we throw tantrums, we behave irrationally (as in spending beyond our means), and we sometimes look around for someone to blame—"My boss doesn't pay me what I'm worth," or "My spouse/children/aged parents are draining me financially."

The steady mushrooming of what we think we require for the good life can be tracked historically. The average size of houses, for example, has grown every decade since World War II, until now "starter castles" are the new norm. (To put this growth in perspective, the average master bedroom has doubled from 130 square feet in the 1950s to 300 square feet today.) Automobiles, despite the accelerating fossil-fuel crisis, have gotten roomier, culminating in the ubiquitous sports utility vehicle and its Frankenstein monster cousin, the Hummer. Food servings at fast-food restaurants have gotten humongous, contributing to the obesity epidemic. In 1968, for example, the average size fountain soda was 8 ounces. Today, customers can slurp up to 128 ounces in a single super serving. And cell phones, smartphones, iPads, Kindles, BlackBerries, and other such gizmos have become so common that we feel lost if we leave home without one or the other (or sometimes two or three) of them. Just a few years ago we were all perfectly satisfied with corner phone booths if we needed to make a call when away from home.

"Gimme this day my daily stuff"

It's absurd to suppose that the habitual patterns we follow day in and day out have no influence on our spiritual lives.

Of course they do. To claim otherwise is at best a naive form of dualism and at worst self-serving denial. So it should come as no surprise that many of us carry the consumer gimme mentality over into our religious lives. We become Genieites, worshipers of an idolatrous deity whose sacred symbol is a shopping mall with stores that cater to every taste. Demanding consumers that we are, we don't hesitate to request even the most embarrassingly mundane gifts of Genie god. We've moved beyond merely asking for abstractions like world peace and graduated to specific requests like cash, new homes, new cars, jewelry, designer handbags, job promotions, and vacations. According to Gloria Copeland, co-prophet with her husband Kenneth for a variety of Genie-god worship known as the "gospel of prosperity," these and other "blessings" are to be had for the asking. "God knows where the money is," she preaches to her followers, "and he knows how to get the money to you."[2] Saint Teresa thought no request too great to take to God. For the Copelands and other devotees of Genie god, no request is too small-minded.

But Genieites like the Copelands or other gospel of prosperity preachers like Jerry Savelle, who tells his followers that the Genie god has a "stimulus package" for them,[3] are small potatoes compared to the man who's become the Genie god's high priest: Bruce Wilkerson. In 1990, Wilkerson published a small book entitled *The Prayer of Jabez,* in which he assured readers that God wanted them to be prosperous and that all their wishes for worldly success would be granted if they took seriously a prayer uttered by Jabez, a figure mentioned just once in the entire Hebrew Bible (and only in passing, during the recitation of one of those tediously long "begat" sections). Jabez, whose name means "he makes sorry," appears in two short verses (1 Chron 4:9–10). Apparently dissatisfied

---

[2] Gloria Copeland, preaching at Southwest Believers' Convention, Fort Worth, Texas, quoted in Laurie Goodstein, "Believers Invest in the Gospel of Getting Rich," *New York Times*, August 15, 2009.

[3] Ibid.

with the fact that his name seems to have stacked the cards against him from birth, Jabez uttered the following short and perfectly inoffensive prayer: "Oh that you would bless me and enlarge my border, and that your hand might be with me, and that you would keep me from hurt and harm!" "And God," we're told, "granted what he asked."

In Wilkerson's deft hands, Jabez's innocent prayer becomes a magic incantation for coaxing Genie god out of his lamp. Regular recitation of the prayer, Wilkerson promises readers, will bring "miraculous power in your life now." And it's pretty clear that the power he's talking about—this is the take-away message that made his little book a runaway bestseller—is the ability to talk Genie god into letting us run loose in the mall. "If Jabez had worked on Wall Street," writes Wilkerson, "he might have prayed, 'Lord, increase the value of my investment portfolios.'. . . When Christian executives ask me, 'Is it right for me to ask God for more business?' my response is 'Absolutely!' If you're doing your business God's way, it's not only right to ask for more, but He is waiting for you to ask."[4]

Wilkerson's devotion to the Genie god has worked out well for him. He's made a fortune from book royalties and consulting fees, and for a while a Jabez industry whose product line included Jabez journals, Jabez devotionals, Jabez Bible studies, and Jabez teen guides flourished. His own success only underscores his message for the thousands of Genieites eager to believe it. When he insists that "seeking God's blessings is our ultimate act of worship," he's singing their song.[5]

Getting what you want

Wilkerson's ninety-page book is really an instruction manual, as its back cover states, on how "to ask God for the abundant blessings He longs to give you." Its recommended way

[4] Bruce Wilkerson, *The Prayer of Jabez: Breaking Through to the Blessed Life* (Sisters, OR: Multnomah, 2000), 92, 31.
[5] Ibid., 49.

of rubbing the lamp is a thirty-day regimen of praying the Jabez petition until it becomes ingrained as the silent mantra that inspires the aspirant's outlook and actions in the world. If you simply *believe*, Wilkerson teaches, it will be so. If you build it, Genie god will come.

But there are many other ways to supplicate Genie god, and his devotees make good use of them all. Moreover, worshipers of this idol are pragmatic. If one strategy for coaxing what they want out of their god doesn't pay off, they move on to other ones. A conscientious consumer never passes up a better deal if one appears.

The strategy that comes most naturally to Genieites is simply asking outright for what they want. As we've already seen, there's nothing intrinsically amiss about making requests of God. It's the manner in which Genieites ask that makes all the difference. In the first place, the request isn't born from an innocent trust or humble hope in divine providence so much as a me-first sense of entitlement. The Genieite is the consumer, and God is the clerk behind the counter whose primary job description is to hand over whatever is asked for quickly and courteously. Genieites may be pragmatic, but they're also an impatient lot. They know what they want, and they want it now. God's responsibility is to serve it up with miraculous swiftness, just as Aladdin's genie instantaneously granted wishes. As we've seen, petulance and anger predictably set in when the request isn't answered right away. Think of the rude guy at the fast food counter who throws a tantrum because he thinks he's waited too long for his burger.

When the twitch of impatience is felt, Genieites ramp up the pressure on their god by resorting to magical incantations or formulas. Of course, they don't think of them as magical. Instead, they see them as signs of their devotion. A rapid-fire clicking of rosary beads, frenetic genuflections, breathlessly repetitious recitations of the Jesus Prayer: these are some of the ways in which devotees of Genie god try to conjure him into granting their wishes. Needless to say, the mindful and reflective use of a Rosary or the Jesus Prayer is a perfectly legitimate devotion. But the Genieite's approach is compulsive, not unlike the overwhelming need of a neurotic to refrain from stepping on sidewalk cracks. He may tell himself that he's simply praying, but in fact he's trying to bend his god's will by whipping up a tornado of irresistible magical energy. Any petitioner who prays to God obviously hopes that God will listen and respond. But the Genieite aims to force his god's hand. There's a big difference.

If the magic isn't bringing in the results he wants, the Genieite can do one of two things. He can accelerate the rituals or incantations—crawling up cathedral steps on his knees, standing in cruciform pose for hours on end, praying through the entire cycle of psalms in a twenty-four hour period—or he can enlist the help of a more powerful magician. Sometimes the Genieite asks a clergyperson or an especially pious layperson to pray on his behalf; at other times, he beseeches "official" saints to intercede for him. Again, what distinguishes his behavior from that of non-idolatrous worshipers is the manner in which he solicits help. He doesn't do so out of a sense of humility or unworthiness—out of the conviction, as a prayer from the Anglican Book of Common Prayer puts it, that he "is not worthy so much as to gather up the crumbs under [God's] table"—but rather out of a presumptuous spirit of connivance. His aim is to out-man Genie god by pulling together an assembly of wizards.

If the magic still doesn't kick in, a Genieite will frequently switch tactics, moving from demanding to bargaining, agreeing to give up something in exchange for something. This quid quo pro attempt to cozy up to a recalcitrant god reeks of consumerism: I give you something, and I get something in return. Like all smart consumers, the Genie god devotee wants to make sure that in the exchange, he comes out on the better end of the stick. So his first offer is something he can easily afford: forgoing that second latte at the corner coffee boutique, cutting back on cussing, getting to church more regularly, tossing a few more dollars in the collection plate. If he needs to, he'll bid higher. But only if he must.

The interesting thing about the quid pro quo tactic to get Genie god out of his lamp is that the devotee almost never really expects to have to pay up in the end. He's like the child who swears, "If I just get this *one* thing, I'll *never* ask for anything else." But, of course, she will. She knows it and her parents know it, so the transaction is an empty ritual. Similarly, most Genieites, habituated as they are to thinking of their god as the great provider, can't really take the deals he offers seriously. They're so positive that Genie god will indulgently smile and forgive their debt that they never bargain in good faith.

Still, some devotees *do* take the quid pro quo seriously under the working assumption that you get what you pay for. So if Genie god doesn't come through on his end of the deal, they feel especially cheated, much as they would if a prepaid online catalog order failed to come in the mail. The playwright Peter Shaffer unforgettably captures this sense of outrage in *Amadeus,* an imaginative portrayal of the relationship between Mozart and his eighteenth-century contemporary, the composer Antonio Salieri.

In Shaffer's play Salieri confesses to the audience that even as a boy he dreamt of becoming a famous composer and escaping the backwater village in which he was born. His fear of not attaining his heart's desire reached such a fever pitch that finally, at the age of sixteen, he "knelt before the God of Bargains" and prayed. "Signore," he implored, "let me be a composer! Grant me sufficient fame to enjoy it. In return, I will live with virtue. I will strive to better the lot of my fellows. And I will honor You with much music all the days of my life."

On finishing his plea, Salieri rose with the conviction that the bargain has been struck. As he grew into manhood and acquired musical fame—confirmation, in his mind, that Genie god was on his side—he kept his end of the bargain. But when the youthful Mozart arrived on the scene and Salieri listened to his music, he instantly realized that Mozart, not he, was the real composer of genius. He felt duped and betrayed by

Genie god, and with a childlike petulance primed by adult
rage he repudiated his idol—not because he finally saw it
for the false god it is, but because it didn't give him what he
wanted. *"Dio ingiusto!"* he shouted. "You are the Enemy! I
name Thee now—*Nemico Eterno!* And this I swear: To my
last breath I shall block You on earth as far as I am able!"[6]

A tactic of final resort that Genieites use to get what they
want out of their god is shaming and demanding. They berate
him for not doing right by them, and they demand—*as a matter of justice, dammit!*—that he begin pulling his weight and
giving them their due. The shaming stage usually goes something like this: "Why are you doing this *to* me/not doing this
for me? What have I done to deserve this/not getting this?"
Then the follow-up punchline: "You *owe* me this!"

It's neither uncommon nor, I think, out of bounds to feel
angry at God sometimes. The biblical Job is the prototype for
anyone who, perplexed by what seems to be God's callous
toying with his life, shakes a defiant fist at the heavens and
demands an explanation. (Whoever talks about the patience
of Job obviously hasn't read the story carefully.) Abraham and
Moses also faced off with God when they disagreed with divine plans, and the Hebrew prophets often followed suit. Elie
Wiesel tells the haunting story of an extraordinary rabbinical
assembly in one of the Nazi death camps that found God
guilty of crimes against humanity for allowing the Holocaust.[7]

But there's a crucial difference between this kind of God-
directed anger and the fury felt by a frustrated Genieite. Job's
sense of injustice is totally righteous. The prologue to the book
of Job makes it perfectly clear that he *is* an innocent man and
that the misery he suffers is deserved in no way. When the
prophets challenged God's intention to inflict violence upon

[6] Peter Shaffer, *Amadeus* (New York: Harper Perennial, 2001), 12,
74–75.

[7] For the story, see Elie Wiesel, *The Trial of God* (New York:
Schocken, 1995). Wiesel sets the trial in the seventeenth century, while
the haunting 2008 film *God on Trial,* directed by Andy DeEmmony,
situates the trial back in Auschwitz.

a group of people or the rabbis condemned God's refusal to forestall evil, they did so not out of selfish motives but out of compassion for suffering humanity. The exclusive concern of Genieites, on the other hand, is themselves—*their* satisfaction, *their* happiness, *their* contentment. It never crosses their minds that there might be more pressing matters in the universe than getting what they want from their idol.

Hungry ghosts and anchors

A few years ago an extraordinary book appeared that diagnosed a cultural malady. The book was named after the illness it described: *Affluenza*. Affluenza, as the book's authors define it, is "a painful, contagious, socially transmitted condition of overload, debt, anxiety, and waste resulting from the dogged pursuit of more."[8] Although a person can come down with the sickness at any time, affluenza season generally falls between Thanksgiving and Christmas, when the entire nation goes on a feverish spending spree.

If affluenza is material consumerism gone viral, spiritual affluenza is the bug bred by the religious consumerism practiced by Genie-god devotees. Like sufferers of material affluenza, Genieites are driven to want more and more because of their fear of doing without, compounded by anxiety over losing what they already have. They become victims of their own desires, forever craving but never fulfilled. Their sad lot is not unlike that of "hungry ghosts," miserable spirits in the Tibetan Buddhist tradition whose rapacious and unappeasable appetites make them, as one commentator puts is, "fusions of rage and desire . . . tormented by unfulfilled cravings and insatiably demanding impossible satisfactions."[9] The differ-

---

[8] John de Graaf, David Wann, and Thomas H. Naylor, *Affluenza: The All-Consuming Epidemic*, 2nd ed. (San Francisco: Berrett-Koehler, 2005), 2. A film by the same name, narrated by National Public Radio's Scott Simon and first aired on PBS, is also available.

[9] Mark Epstein, *Thoughts Without a Thinker: Psychotherapy from a Buddhist Perspective* (New York: Basic Books, 1995), 28.

ence, of course, is that hungry ghosts are mythical creatures. Genieites, who are what psychologist Erich Fromm once called "consumption-hungry," are very real indeed.[10]

The way to avoid affluenza, either the material or spiritual variety, isn't to quell desire. On the material front, it's both natural and good that we desire food and drink, shelter and companionship, because we need them to survive physically. On the spiritual front, properly directed desire leads us to what we genuinely need as opposed to what we merely want. All of our desires, no matter how frivolous they may be, are fueled by the mother of all desires: a yearning for that which will complete us, for something beyond ourselves that transcends our specific tastes and temperamental cravings. It is a longing for deep Reality. This "repining restlesnesse," as the poet George Herbert put it, is the "pulley" that eventually raises us to God if we but let it. It is the spiritual umbilical cord that keeps us forever connected to the Source of our being.[11]

But the devotee of Genie god doesn't realize either the source or the target of her desire. Lulled by the consumer culture in which she's immersed, she believes that what she really wants are all the commodities she's been programmed to believe will give her the good life. In her obsessive fear of doing without them, she never takes the time to examine the nature of the underlying desire exploited and misdirected by the market. If she did, she would discover that her desire is a blessing and gift from God that she's called to treasure and nurture. Instead, her desire gets twisted into an addiction that drives her away from the God of joy and fulfillment to the suffocating embrace of Genie god. The very desire God intends to be a pulley becomes an anchor.

---

[10] Fromm, *The Sane Society,* 135.
[11] George Herbert (1598–1633), "The Pulley."

Chapter 3

Big Brother god

I am a worm, and no man.

—Psalm 22:6

*O you hypocrites, O you whited sep-
ulchers, O you who present a smooth
smiling face to the world while your
soul within is a foul swamp of sin,
how will it fare with you in that terrible day?*

—Father Arnall[1]

The term "Big Brother" is widely known in the English-speak-
ing world. It comes, of course, from George Orwell's *1984,*
a novel about the fictional totalitarian society of Oceania, in
which the surveillance of the dictator, Big Brother, intrudes
everywhere. From thousands of cameras captioned with the
warning "Big Brother Is Watching You!" strategically placed
in subways, cafes, workplaces, and apartments, he scrutinizes
the public and private lives of Oceanians, ready to pounce at
their slightest infraction. Big Brother is so ubiquitous that he's

---

[1] Father Arnall's fire-and-brimstone sermon, in James Joyce, *A
Portrait of the Artist as a Young Man* (Mineola, NY: Dover, 1994), 81.

taken on a larger-than-life mythic status in his subjects' minds. No one quite remembers any longer when he was born, and they're beginning to suspect, as one of the novel's characters puts it, that he will never die. Big Brother is now and always will be watching, so prudent citizens walk the straight and narrow. In the hope of staying on his good side, they're not above spying and informing on relatives and neighbors.

The ever-present and baleful scrutiny of Big Brother (reminiscent, by the way, of the piercing gaze of the Eye of Saurin in Tolkien's *Lord of the Rings* epic) has become a symbol of totalitarian repression. When civil libertarians worry about governmental encroachment on private lives, they invoke the specter of Big Brother. Literate adolescents chafing under household rules sometimes angrily refer to their parents as Big Brother. The relentless voyeurism associated with the term apparently fascinates us, even inspiring popular entertainment such as the film "The Truman Show" and the reality television program "Big Brother."

But long before Orwell coined the expression, people worshiped a god made in the image of Big Brother. Some idols are comfortable with a live-and-let-live policy toward their competitors. But not Big Brother god. He jealously demands absolute loyalty from his followers. Big Brother god lays down strict rules that he expects to be obeyed to the letter. He's always on the lookout for missteps, and nothing slips past him. His devotees feel the constant weight of his gaze. Some of them get crushed by the burden. Others, out of sheer self-defense, deflect their god's judgmental scrutiny away from themselves and onto others. To curry his favor, they condemn others in his name, self-righteously spewing fire-and-brimstone jeremiads against individual trespasses and human wickedness in general. The burnt offering they lay before Big Brother god is the crackling of sinners in hell.

In many ways Big Brother god is the polar opposite of Genie god. As we saw in the last chapter, Genieites believe that their deity can be schmoozed into giving them whatever they want. Big Brother god isn't such an easy mark. Instead of giving, he demands. To invoke a well-known refrain from a popular song that's supposed to be cheery but comes across as downright creepy if you actually listen to its words:

> He knows when you've been sleeping,
> He knows when you're awake,
> He knows when you've been good or bad
> So be good for goodness sake!
> Oh, you better watch out . . .

So far as Big Brother god is concerned, no one is ever good. Coal in the stocking is always the order of the day.

Burnt offerings

As we saw in Chapter 1, freedom is a precious but also threatening gift. Those of us fearful of accepting it (and let's face it, that's most of us at one time or another) resort to any number of strategies for walking away from it. The way Big Brother–god devotees evade freedom is by locking themselves into a universe so densely criss-crossed with moral, sexual, behavioral, and religious dos and don'ts that there's no wiggle room left for choice. Their idol's primary selling point is that he does their thinking for them, absolving them of the burden of making decisions. All they have to do is follow the heavenly rule book and things will go well; they'll live happy lives, be good people, and go to heaven when they die. Big Brother god loves a team player.

That's the up side of their cult. The down side is that Big Brother god's rule book is either too complicated to understand or too demanding for anyone to live up to. The moment one becomes a devotee of Big Brother god, she dooms herself to failure. He simply requires more than even the most scrupulous human beings can deliver.

Some Big Brotherites are progressively crushed by the religious vise they put themselves in. The more frightened of decision making they are, the more rules they need their god to hand down to them. But the more rules there are to follow, the more impossible the task of obeying them becomes. So Big Brother devotees grow steadily more convinced that they're unworthy of their god because they can't possibly adhere to all the regulations that, ironically, they hoped would safely regulate and order their lives. It's a quick downhill slide from there to the bleak valley of remorseful self-loathing. And because they believe that their god is always watching and judging them, they can't help but assume that he loathes them too. It's a terrible price to pay for avoiding freedom—one that a reasonable person surely would reject—but Big Brotherites generally are incapable of seeing this. They just sink lower and lower under the weight of guilt, shame, and self-contempt, ever more desperately trying and failing to live up to their deity's expectations.

A sociologist might explain the dynamic responsible for this self-loathing by appealing to the looking-glass theory of identity. According to it, our sense of self is formed by what we think others think of us. The judgments others make about me, which I pick up on by observing the expressions on their faces as well as the ways they treat me, are mirrors or looking glasses in which I see what I take to be my true reflection. Sooner or later, especially if the others' opinions are important to me, I internalize their judgments of who I am. I begin to see myself through their eyes.

For the Big Brotherite, his god is the supreme looking-glass other—the only one, in fact, whose opinion really matters. And Big Brother is always frowning. Given that the devotee will never be able to satisfy Big Brother demands, he'll always feel negatively judged by him. But to reject or defy his god's disappointment would actually be to exercise the freedom he dreads. So he meekly accepts and internalizes failure. In his own eyes—as, he believes, in the eyes of his god—he's a loser.

Perhaps the most obvious example of a Big Brother idolater who unhealthily internalized the unforgiving scrutiny of his looking-glass god is Saul, who eventually became the apostle

Paul. As a good Pharisee in first-century Palestine, he strove hard to conform to the 613 *mizvot* or commandments laid down in the Torah. These laws regulated how to think and speak about God, how to dress, what to eat, how to relate to fellow Jews as well as Gentiles, when to rest and when to work, when to have sex, how to settle civil and criminal grievances, and so on. Everything was set down in black-letter law, leaving no ambiguity, no doubt, and no need to ponder. What could be simpler, what could be more straightforward, than this ready-made set of formulaic instructions for righteousness?

Yet Saul felt increasingly oppressed by the demands of the law. Years afterward, Paul described his youthful frustration to the Christians in Rome, most of whom probably had no firsthand familiarity with the tightly regulated universe from which he came. Paul recounted for them the supreme irony of his old life: trying to please God by obeying every jot and tittle of the law only resulted in inevitable violations of the law, which, of course, displeased God. The very laws themselves, in other words, encouraged law breaking. The moment they were accepted as standards, the slightest transgression of them counted as sin: "For sin," as Paul wrote, always finds "an opportunity in the commandment" (Rom 7:11). So his youth was a whirlwind of conflict in which the 613 Pharisaic laws vied with Paul's natural urges, driving him ever further away from obedience to the law until he finally cried in despair: "Wretched man that I am! Who will rescue me from this body of death?" (Rom 7:24). Crushed by such self-loathing and guilt, it's no surprise that Saul eventually suffered a mental and spiritual collapse on his way to Damascus.

Now, what I'm most definitely *not* saying here is that first-century Pharisees and contemporary Orthodox and Conservative Jews are worshipers of Big Brother god. All religious believers, whatever their traditions, accept that God proscribes some actions, requires others, and is indifferent to still others. Honoring God means in part trying hard to live reflectively and consistently within certain moral boundaries.

The believer accepts this task, both to testify to her trusting love of God and in the confidence that conforming her will to God's will is the high road to genuine happiness.

But some believers, because of their particular temperamental needs, obsessively transform what should be an act of loving and freely chosen submission into one of self-destructive subservience. In doing so, they mutate God into unforgiving Big Brother god. For them, guidelines for behavior become lockstep requirements permitting no leeway. Instead of embracing God's commandments as invitations to fulfillment, happiness, and holiness, they compulsively make them fetishes by transforming them into boxes to be ticked off on a performance report. They wind up damaging themselves in their mania for perfection, just as Saul did, because what they desperately want to do— placate their demanding god—is impossible. Their failure not only forces them to live with an unrelenting sense of guilt, but it can also prod them into punishing themselves in a perverse play for Big Brother god's approval. The history of Christianity is sprinkled with guilt-ridden individuals whose self-abuse, even though it may masquerade as devotion, can only be seen as pitiable religious masochism.

The way Saul was crushed by the unachievable demands placed on him by his Big Brother god has been repeated a heartbreaking number of times in the two millennia since he struggled with the 613 laws. Ascetics who regress to a self-hating repudiation of even the most innocent human pleasures; Puritans who suffer under the hopeless obsession that God consigned them to hell aeons before they were even born; guilt-riddled parishioners, all too familiar to every priest and pastor, who hate themselves for "sins" and "transgressions" that no reasonable person—much less God—sees as condemnable; neurotics who fancy that they're the exclusive focus of God's wrathful censure: these are all Big Brotherites who have been devoured by their rapacious deity. Their overwhelming guilt creates a spiritual hypochondria in which they imagine all sorts of faults, shortcomings, and sins that only compound their self-loathing. They declare themselves unworthy of their god's mercy (which is good, since he extends none to them) and lead miserable, unfruitful lives. Like the Psalmist, they grovel in the dust. They are worms.

Venomous serpents

A good number of Big Brother–god devotees come to loathe themselves in this way. But even more of them go in the opposite direction by concluding that everyone else is a venomous serpent. Self-hatred is a difficult emotion to sustain. It's too painful and too debilitating. Most Big Brotherites can't bear its corrosive effects any longer than the rest of us. A few of them ultimately get out from under by mustering the courage to renounce their idol. Some who do have been so bloodied by his demands that they walk away from religion altogether and embrace atheism (which, if they're not careful, can become yet another idol). Others, like Saul, land on their feet, because they discover the living God. They learn from firsthand experience that freedom, scary as it can be, is infinitely more rewarding than enslavement to Big Brother god. But most Big Brotherites adopt a third coping mechanism. They deal with their self-hating sense of inadequacy by displacing it onto others. Acting in the name of their god, they become the scourge of sinners, self-righteously denouncing the rest of humanity in his name. They can find a thousand different ways, ranging from a superciliously raised eyebrow to a frontal verbal assault, to lambast others for their failure to live up to their god's standards. Never mind that they can't either. But by becoming his bulldogs, they both suck up to Big Brother god and deflect their own sense of guilt and self-loathing.

The spirit and tone of the jeremiads these Big Brotherites are capable of launching have been delightfully (and mockingly) captured over the years by some of the world's greatest authors. The roof-raising sermon of Father Arnell in James Joyce's *Portrait of the Artist as a Young Man,* for example, still sends shivers down my spine whenever I read it, not least because I regularly sat through ones like it when I was a boy. There's also Father Mapple's sermon in *Moby Dick,* appropriately delivered during a howling storm, in which he warns his seafaring audience to repent lest they, like Jonah, be swallowed by the maw of an angry god. And then, of course, there's perhaps the most famous jeremiad of all, the real-life one spewed by the American Calvinist Jonathan Edwards in a 1741 sermon entitled "Sinners in the Hands of an Angry God." In it, Edwards terrified his audience by shouting at them that

> the God that holds you over the pit of hell, much as one holds a spider, or some loathsome insect, over the fire, abhors you, and is dreadfully provoked; his wrath toward you burns like fire; he looks upon you as worthy of nothing else, but to be cast into the fire; he is of purer eyes than to bear to have you in his sight; you are ten thousand times so abominable in his eyes as the most hateful venomous serpent is in ours.[2]

But my personal favorite from this reeking-of-sulphur genre comes from an 1879 book entitled *Tracts for Spiritual Reading,* written expressly to prepare children for first communion. In it the author, a Catholic priest, describes various "dungeons" in hell set aside for wicked boys and girls. Here's his description of one of them:

> Look into this little prison. In the middle of it there is a boy, a young man. He is silent; despair is on him. His eyes are burning like two burning coals. Two long flames come out of his ears. His breathing is difficult.

---

[2] For the complete text of Edwards's frightening sermon, see John E. Smith, Harry S. Stout, Kenneth P. Minkema, eds., *A Jonathan Edwards Reader* (New Haven, CT: Yale University Press, 2003). The quoted passage is on page 97.

Sometimes he opens his mouth and breath of blazing fire rolls out of it. But listen! There is a sound just like that of a kettle boiling. Is it really a kettle that is boiling? No; then what is it? Hear what it is. The blood is boiling in the scalding veins of that boy. The brain is boiling and bubbling in his head. The marrow is boiling in his bones. Ask him why he is thus tormented. His answer is that when he was alive, his blood boiled to do very wicked things.[3]

For many of us, this kind of religious rhetoric is so over the top that it comes across as laughable. Certainly James Joyce's intention in writing Father Arnall's sermon was partly to make us chuckle. But we ought to take these jeremiads seriously for at least two reasons. The first is that fire-and-brimstone sermons bewailing the utter depravity of humans and mercilessly consigning them to hell are an undeniable historical reality. Huge swaths of the Christian tradition have displayed unhealthy doses of Big Brotherism, especially since the Protestant Reformation, by obsessively focusing on human fallenness. The second reason is that dour Big Brother judgmentalism is alive and well today in the United States, especially among evangelical Protestants and ultra-conservative Catholics. They may not speak with the eloquence of a Jonathan Edwards or the dignity of a Father Mapple—their delivery, in fact, is often crude and screechy—but their message is the same: society is corrupt, humans are depraved, original sin sullies all human enterprises, disobedience to God is pandemic. To hear them speak, one would never guess that humans are actually made in a good and loving God's likeness.

The extent to which Big Brotherism has infected the American Christian scene is frighteningly obvious if one surfs the

---

[3] The passage from *Tracts for Spiritual Reading* is taken from an unflattering anonymous review of the book in *Methodist Review* (November-December 1894), 941.

thousands of Internet sites that claim to preach the gospel. The overriding impression one gets from many of them is that the good news of a loving communion between God and humanity has been replaced by the bad news of sin, dissolution, apocalyptic doom, and hell. Their inventory of what their god demands and what he forbids is every bit as exhaustive as the ancient catalogue of *mitzvot,* covering every aspect of daily living from speech to sex, lifestyle to music, facial hair to childrearing. And the kicker is this: no matter how hard we try, we just can't help being wicked. "We are all sinners," proclaims an all-too-representative site, proofthat-godexists.org, "first because we inherited the sin of Adam, and secondly because we all fall short of God's requirement to keep his law."

So the bad news according to Big Brotherites is that god disapproves of everything and everyone—well, almost everyone, because they believe that their eagerness to point out the mote in everyone else's eye is an indication that they, despite their own transgressions, have found favor with Big Brother god. They've been "saved." The rest of us haven't, because we rebelliously persevere in our sinful disobedience, ignoring the fact that Big Brother god watches our every move—he knows if we've been good or bad!—and forgets nothing. Still, Big Brother devotees won't slacken in their mission to convince us of our depravity. Their weapon of choice in these enlightened times is the spoken and written word, but the threat of physical persecution lies just beneath the surface of their fire-and-brimstone harangues.

We can turn once more to Saul for an obvious example of this danger. While still a Big Brotherite, he tried to mollify his stern god by projecting his self-hatred on others—namely Christians—whom he considered to be even more sinful than himself. No one was more zealous than Saul in the persecution of Jesus's first followers. He hounded them, railed against them, rounded them up, testified against them, applauded when they were sentenced and executed, traveled outside of Jerusalem to persecute as many as he could lay his hands on, and in general scurried around "breathing threats and murder against the disciples of the Lord" (Acts 9:1). In the process he probably succeeded in shoving to the back of his mind his own sense of unworthiness. After all, it's difficult to imagine a man *consciously* tortured by his own inability to obey divine commandments having the brass to condemn others for the same offense. When he guarded the cloaks of his fellow Big Brotherites as they stoned Stephen to death, Saul must've had a keen sense of his own righteousness, albeit one tinctured by uneasiness.

In his 1957 film *The Seventh Seal* Ingmar Bergman offers another classic portrait of the brutality to which Big Brother idolatry can give rise that's every bit as gripping as the biblical description of persecutor Saul. In the scene I've got in mind, in fact, both types of Big Brother worshipers, those who loathe themselves and those who loathe others, appear side by side. It's a chilling and revealing juxtaposition.

The film is set in medieval Sweden, a land decimated by a plague that most of the characters see as divine punishment for sin. At the height of the epidemic a procession of flagellants wanders from one terrified village to the next, wailing out a message of destruction and doom. Stripped to the waist, they penitently and savagely beat themselves with corded whips and switches to appease their wrathful god. Unable to give Big Brother god the obedience he demands, yet fearful of rebelling against the impossible rules he prescribes, they punish themselves for their failure in the hope that their penance will spare them from the plague. Their masochistic contrition is all the more pathetic because it neither placates their god nor tempers the epidemic's fury one little bit.

Traveling with the flagellants is a hooded monk who launches into a jeremiad in each of the villages the dismal caravan visits. Alternatively mocking and threatening, he tells his audiences that the god whom they've so offended by their unrighteousness is preparing to strike them down at any moment with the horrible sickness devastating the land. The fair maiden, the child at the mother's breast, the wealthy businessman, the village idiot, the pious priest: all have fallen short, and none will be spared. In strange contrast to the terrible words he delivers, the expression on the monk's face is smug, superior, almost triumphant. He clearly takes a perverse pleasure in offering the hapless villagers up to Big Brother god's wrath. And because Bergman puts both the monk and the flagellants in the same scene, the fact that there's a kinship between masochistic self-hatred and the self-righteous condemnation of others comes across loud and clear. The two are different sides of the same idolatrous coin.

Schadenfreude is the technical term for the monk's pleasure at the misery of others. It's a particularly nasty emotion. Thankfully, although most of us experience it from time to time, very few of us are driven by it to the degree that fire-and-brimstone Big Brotherites are. *Schadenfreude* is a frustrated resentment that quickly becomes toxic. Tormented by a persistent sense of inadequacy and unfulfillment, the only source of pleasure left for someone in the grip of *Schadenfreude* is dragging others down to the same level of misery. The Big Brother devotee who displaces his self-loathing onto others may deceive himself into thinking that he's a prophet crying in the wilderness. But, in fact, he's simply trying to cope with his own unhappiness.

An entropic kingdom

Orwell's Oceania is a land of decay, and Big Brother is its presiding Angel of Death. Everything in it reeks of the tomb. Material poverty and squalor are everywhere. Peeling paint, stale aromas, crumbling infrastructure, drab uniforms, and food rationing are the dismal norms. Oceania's spiritual poverty is just as evident. Its citizens waffle among states of fear, confusion, and boredom. If they find any pleasure at all, it's in gloating at the terrific destruction that Big Brother promises to launch against enemies within and without—a collective and reprehensible *Schadenfreude*. The society's spiritual decay is further evidenced by the fact that traditional standards of truth and, startlingly, even fundamental rules of logic are thrown out the window. As Big Brother's telescreens digitally proclaim day and night, "slavery is freedom," "death is life," and "ignorance is knowledge." Oceanians have sunk so low that they're apparently unbothered by such nonsense.

All this adds up to the overwhelming impression that Orwell's horrible new world is a materially and spiritually moribund culture, living off of a power supply that's being used up without being replenished in any way. Oceania, in other words, is an entropic kingdom, slowly growing colder and colder until it reaches the point when all life in it finally flickers out. It may be able to continue for a while from sheer inertia. But it will eventually grind to a halt because its totalitarian lockdown of the human spirit stifles vitality, freedom, and ultimately hope.

The kingdom of Big Brother god is similarly entropic. It lacks a future because its inhabitants have renounced freedom for the sake of lockstep conformity to ironbound rules, and it lacks vitality because the rules are too burdensome to bear. Devotees of Big Brother god are hopeless, seeing no way either to live up to his harsh expectations themselves or to induce others to do so. No wonder the fear that motivates their idolatry leads them to violence against themselves and sometimes others. For Big Brotherites, the parable of the Prodigal Son doesn't register. No forgiving and loving father will embrace them and slaughter the fatted calf. They themselves are the fatted calves offered up to their ravenous god.

The entropic nature of Big Brother idolatry is underscored by the fact that devotees aren't really interested in reforming society or converting the hearts and minds of individuals. Their only mandate is to condemn. Father Arnall, Jonathan Edwards, Bergman's monk: their shared message is an utterly fatalistic one of fallenness, destruction, and doom, not rebirth. Because they're unable to live up to their god's rigid and multitudinous rules, they conclude (quite correctly, by the way) that no one else can either. Given that, what else is there to do but thunderously condemn, so that at least everyone who hears them will become as hopeless as they are? Ultimately, this is what their god demands. If he can't have obedience, he insists on sackcloth, ashes, and perpetual twilight.

Of all the forms of idolatry explored in this book, Big Brotherism strikes me as the saddest. Members of the cult, for all their fear of freedom, must feel utterly trapped by the unloving god to whom they've given themselves over. In their equally unloving service to him, those who sink into masochistic self-loathing sacrifice any sense of dignity or worth, while those who project their self-hatred against others cut themselves off from the comforts of human fellowship. The perverse satisfaction that comes from *Schadenfreude* is too small a compensation for this kind of exile. Worship of Big Brother god blights everything.

To make things worse, Big Brotherites are less likely than worshipers of other idols to escape their god's clutches. The temperamental timidity that attracted them to him in the first place is only likely to deepen as they discover their absolute inability to live up to his demands. Masochistic devotees soon lose whatever self-confidence they once had; fire-and-brimstone ones grow too reliant on anaesthetizing their own unhappiness by serving as hurtful instruments of their wrathful god. For both, leaving their god becomes progressively difficult. Like abused spouses, they stay because they can see no way out and, more fundamentally, because they believe that they deserve their suffering. The Sauls who break free of Big Brother god to become radically new persons are, I fear, few and far between.

Chapter 4

Patriot god

We salute you, land of liberty;
You're the choicest land on earth.
We salute you, land of liberty;
You're the land of priceless worth.
Keep wide the gates of freedom,
to people great and small.
We salute you, land of liberty;
you are the greatest land of all.

—FRANK GARLOCK[1]

JesUSAves

—BUMPER STICKER

At one point in the 2011 movie *The Ides of March,* candidate
for the Democratic presidential nomination Mike Morris
(played by the talented George Clooney) is pressed in a public
debate to declare his religious beliefs. He resists responding,
but his opponent refuses to drop the issue. So Morris spills

---

[1] Frank Garlock, "We Salute You, Land of Liberty," in *Praises III*
(Greenville, SC: Majesty Music, 1991). This volume is the third in a
series of patriotic/praise music.

the beans. "I am not a Christian or an atheist," he says. "I'm not Jewish or a Muslim. What I believe, my religion, is written on a piece of paper called the Constitution."

On the one hand, there's something refreshing about Morris's candor in a day and age when candidates for elected office feel obliged to offer splashy and often overdone assurances about their religious credentials. His refusal to pander is courageous, and the promise he makes a couple of lines later, to protect constitutionally guaranteed religious liberties, is admirable. Morris comes across as a guy who just might make a good president.

And yet, on the other hand, there's something disconcerting about his claim that the Constitution is his religion. Respecting it as the nation's single most significant codification of governmental responsibility and citizen rights is fine. The same goes for defending its principles when they're in jeopardy or under assault. But claiming it as an ultimate concern, the foundational principle and primary value from which all other principles and values are generated, seems to go too far. It bestows upon the document, and by implication the nation that birthed it, an authority that properly belongs only to God. It gestures at idolatry.

Now, it could simply be that when Morris says the Constitution is his religion, he's indulging in a bit of rhetorical hyperbole to underscore his commitment to law and order. But his remark reminds us that there are many people in this and other countries throughout the world whose patriotic devotion to their native land is so strong that it really *is* their religion. To their mind, God has blessed their nation, singled it out as the best and the choicest, and destined it to lead the rest of the world. Their country's prosperity doesn't just please God but is actually a reflection of God's will. For them, in fact, patriotism gets so fused with religious sensibilities and rhetoric, whether Christianity in the United States, Islam in Afghanistan, or Judaism in Israel, that it becomes impossible to separate the two. They are "patriolaters," and the deity they worship wears a robe decorated with the stars and stripes, a crescent, a star of David. He is Patriot god, and he's a very dangerous god indeed.

Nation worship

There's nothing wrong with patriotism, if it means love and loyalty to what's best in one's national heritage. A genuine patriot acknowledges that his country is capable of embracing suspect values at times, enacting laws that unfairly privilege one group over another, or adopting overly aggressive foreign policies. He has no patience with the claim that something is automatically good simply because it's endorsed by his country's government or people, or is in the "national interest." For him, national policy must be weighed against moral principles, not the other way around. The genuine patriot, in other words, sees, celebrates, and wishes to nurture his country's best qualities. But he doesn't allow his vision of what his country *might* be to blind him to any of its actual blemishes. His patriotism demands that he speak out against immoral policies or courses of action, and sometimes even engage in civil disobedience. A "love it or leave it" option simply isn't in his playbook. Antebellum American abolitionists, German resisters to the Third Reich, Soviet dissidents, Wall Street occupiers: all of them acted out of loyalty to a moral vision of what their countries could be. They were genuine patriots.

"Patriolatry," a perverse caricature of patriotism, rests on the conviction that the nation's legal and cultural norms are the absolute standards for all moral judgments. Love and loyalty to country are indiscriminate and unqualified. Any policy enacted by the nation is considered praiseworthy simply by virtue of the fact that it's "ours." Domestic customs become the standards against which foreign norms are judged and typically disparaged. When the patriolater observes that "that's how *they* do things," it's always with a note of contempt. National chauvinism can be militantly secular, as with

Soviet totalitarianism or Chinese Maoism, although even then intense devotion to state and the cult of personality took on a faux-religious fervor. Pius XI certainly thought so when he referred to secular nationalism in 1931 as "a true, a real pagan worship of the State."[2] But patriolatry overtly fuses with religious belief. National interests become identified with divine providence, which in turns nurtures the conviction that any policy or action that strengthens the nation is ipso facto blessed by God. When this mixture of religion and nationalism happens, political rhetoric begins to take on a religious flavor, national holidays get treated with the solemnity of holy days, statesmen and soldiers acquire near sainthood status, and opposition to the country's policies is condemned not merely as traitorous but vaguely blasphemous. Once a "*Gott mit uns*" atmosphere sets in, whoever disagrees "*mit uns*" also defies "*Gott.*"

Devotees of Patriot god probably can be found in any country, but they seem particularly on the rise in the United States. They began to assert themselves with the creation of the Moral Majority in 1979, and their numbers surged after the 9/11 terrorist attacks in New York, Washington DC, and Pennsylvania. The growth is particularly apparent in one demographic group: white evangelicals, who as a whole tend to be politically conservative (70 percent, for example, identify themselves as members of the Republican Party).[3] A 2010 survey unsurprisingly found that nearly 80 percent of white evangelicals think that "God has granted America a special role in human history."[4] Another survey conducted the following year revealed that 69 percent of people who identify as members of the religious right endorse the political aims

---

[2] For Pius XI's warning about what he called "statolatry," see *Non abbiamo bisogno* (1931), no. 44. All official church documents are available on the vatican.va website.

[3] "Lift Every Voice," *The Economist* (May 5, 2012).

[4] Proofthatgodexists.org, quoted in Ross Douthat, *Bad Religion: How We Became a Nation of Heretics* (New York: Free Press, 2012), 250.

of the Tea Party movement.[5] They're also the same demographic group most likely to display the American flag on their clothing, at home, or in church; to support constitutional amendments to criminalize misuse of the flag; to reintroduce prayer in public schools; and to endorse evangelical political candidates.

As I mentioned earlier, the peculiar fusion of nation and religion endorsed by patriolaters bestows a sacred status upon national holidays, heroes, and emblems. Patriot god devotees in the United States celebrate Memorial Day, Veterans Day, and the Fourth of July with a sometimes bewildering mixture of religious solemnity and high-spirited partying. Emblems such as the American eagle or the American flag become, in the words of one legal scholar, "the equivalent of a sacred religious icon, comparable to Christianity's crucifix, Judaism's Torah and the Koran of Islam."[6] Just as church altars and holy sites can be desecrated by unbelievers, so patriolaters believe the American flag can be as well. Songs such as the "Star Spangled Banner" ("Praise the Power that hath made and preserved us a nation/Then conquer we must, when our cause it is just") and "America" ("God shed his grace on thee!") become more than testimonies to love of country; they're first and foremost religious hymns. Saying the Pledge of Allegiance ("one nation, under God") becomes the recitation of a religious creed. Presidents' Day carries the spiritual weight of a saint's feast day. To refuse to recite the Pledge of Allegiance, to criticize military pomp and circumstance on Independence Day, or to remain seated and silent during the singing of the national anthem is an act of disrespect that evokes quick and loud censure. One commentator concludes that even though "no court has designated patriotism as a

---

[5] Scott Clement and John C. Green, "The Tea Party, Religion, and Social Issues," *Pew Forum on Religion and Public Life* (February 23, 2011).

[6] Muriel Morisey, "Flag Desecration, Religion, and Patriotism," *Rutgers Journal of Law and Religion* 9 (Fall 2007): 1.

religion for Establishment Clause purposes . . . in every other significant respect it operates as a religion in American culture." It's hard to know how far to generalize this observation. But it fits Patriot-god devotees to a tee.[7]

One of the foundational dogmas embraced by American patriolaters is that the United States was founded on biblical values and that the founding fathers intended the nation to be Christian (with *Christian* usually meaning evangelical Protestant). Devotees generally hotly deny historical evidence to the contrary—for example, that there was no consensus of religious belief among the founders, that many of them were obviously deists rather than Christians, and that no mention of the Christian God is in the founding documents—because doing so would fly in the face of their insistence that America has been specially chosen by God. For them, divinely ordained American exceptionalism is in constant danger of corruption by a secular-led drift away from biblical values. So to placate their deity and retain his special affection for America, devotees of Patriot god are always on the lookout for heretics, apostates, and infidels. The jeremiads they hurl at them nearly always predict doom and destruction unless the nation turns away from godlessness and re-embraces its evangelical heritage. Like Big Brotherites, patriolaters are good at pseudo-prophetic invective.

Fortresses and crusades

Patriot-god worshipers, especially ones who are also citizens of economically and militarily powerful nations, see themselves as superior, privileged beings who occupy the moral high ground or, better, the holy mountain. They're not shy about condemning fellow citizens who don't buy into their idolatry, and we've already seen that they're contemptuous of the values, religious beliefs, and customs of other nations. Why wouldn't they be? If the deity especially favors their

---

[7] Ibid., 2.

nation, then it's obvious that domestic dissenters are in error and foreign cultures suspect. Their myopic sense of community includes the elect—their fellow countrymen, or at least the right-thinking ones—and pretty much excludes everyone else. As a consequence, devotees of Patriot god have a low threshold when it comes to tolerating differences.

But their arrogance is partly a defense mechanism. Zealous true believers who preach and practice intolerance frequently do so to compensate for their own anxieties. What Patriot-god idolaters fear above all else is the vulnerability of no longer being special. To believe that "God shed his grace" upon one's country, thereby setting it and its citizens qualitatively apart from the rest of the world, is to attribute exceptional meaning and value to one's own existence. It's a heady self-esteem enhancer. No matter how low someone is in the pecking order, he's still special if he belongs to a nation that is God's handpicked favorite. Compared to people from other countries, even the ones who are rich and powerful, he's one of the elect. Moreover, believing that one's nation has been singled out by the deity permits the acceptance, with clear conscience, of national policies that might otherwise raise pesky moral doubts, anxiety, or indecision. It excuses the Patriot-god devotee from hard thinking and self-examination when it comes to values and normative convictions. This is important, because without his confidence that God favors his nation above all others, the devotee would lose his comfortably secure sense of superiority. The love God has for him would turn out to be no greater than the love God has for everyone else, regardless of their nation of birth, and this is a leveling of the playing field that the patriolater can't tolerate. The thought of such a fall from grace keeps him up at night.

But a Patriot-god devotee's sense of exceptionalism comes with a price. His conviction that his country is singularly blessed by God means that he sees himself surrounded by an entire world of fallen nations and peoples. He tends to slip into a state-of-siege mentality, convinced that dangerous enemies are on every side. He firmly believes that "they" hate everything he stands for and mean to do harm to him, the nation, and his god if they can. For the patriolater, the list of people in the "they" category is long and forever growing: atheists, feminists, liberal Christians, political liberals, evolutionists, weather scientists, homosexuals, illegal immigrants, Jews, Muslims, Shiites, Sunnis, and so on. The immorality of these outsiders is a continuous affront to Patriot god and risks stirring up his wrath—yet something else to worry about. Patriolaters in the United States suspect that the "sins" of homosexuality and membership in the ACLU caused the terrorist attacks of 9/11 (so Jerry Falwell and Pat Robertson announced immediately thereafter) and Hurricane Katrina (so said John Hagee, the Texas-based fundamentalist pastor).

Faced with this sense of constant danger to their way of life, it's no surprise that patriolaters can reach the point where they feel it's not enough to keep vigilant guard on the ramparts. Sometimes it's necessary to attack the evil that challenges their god and threatens their way of life. So the fortress gates that keep the bad world at bay periodically swing open and the minions of Patriot-god's army march forth under a sacred banner—which is the same as their national flag. Doing battle against enemies within and without, Patriot-god soldiers fight not only to protect themselves, but also to convert as much of the rest of the world as they can. They believe they have a mandate to remodel the world in conformity with what they see as a godly way of life, which of course means their *national* way of life.

Armed with this conviction, devotees of Patriot god often rev themselves up into declaring crusades against foreign and domestic wickedness. At the individual and local levels, the crusades usually are wars of words carried out in letters to the editor, public prayer rallies, and pulpits. The zealous absolutism characteristic of crusades thickens the air with tension and recrimination but thankfully expresses itself in nonviolent, or at least nonphysical, ways.

In our media age it's not uncommon for patriolatrous crusades that in an earlier time would've stayed local to go nationwide. The most recent notable one in the United States was launched in 2010 by conservative radio and television celebrity Glenn Beck. Called the Restoring Honor Rally, it was held at the Lincoln Memorial in Washington DC. Tens of thousands either attended in person or watched on televisions and computers. The rally was a perfect fusion of patriotic jingoism and evangelical Christian revivalism. Alveda King, daughter of civil rights leader Martin Luther King, Jr., gave a particularly impassioned sermon in which she married Bible and Constitution, and the whole event was climaxed by a rambling exhortation on Beck's part for America to return to faith and restore the nation to its God-ordained place as leader of the world. He spoke in front of three huge banners—icons, really—of founding fathers John Adams, George Washington, and Ben Franklin, each captioned with "Faith," "Hope," and "Charity," the three traditional theological virtues. People in the crowd wore American flag shirts and Uncle Sam top hats, waved crosses and small American flags, and held signs that praised US troops, remembered the victims of 9/11, and urged the nation to turn to God. Many of them raised placards advertising a website (now closed) called ChristianNationNow.com., a name that perfectly summed up the spirit behind the rally. Just a few months later Beck publicly warned his listeners against false Christian sects that betrayed both Patriot god and the nation with their "socialist" teachings. "I beg you," he said, "look for the words 'social justice' or 'economic justice' on your church Web site. If you find it, run as fast as you can. Social justice and economic justice, they are code words"—presumably of the anti-Christ.[8]

---

[8] Tobin Grant, "Glenn Beck: 'Leave Your Church,'" *Christianity Today* (March 12, 2010). Beck made his offending plea on the March 2 broadcast of his radio show. He was immediately called to task by dozens of religious leaders from both ends of the political spectrum.

But political and religious liberalism isn't the only enemy patriolaters spy just outside (and inside) the gates. Since 9/11, worldwide Islam in general and American Muslims in particular have also been relegated by US devotees of Patriot god to the "they" category. Domestic hate crimes against Muslims (or in some cases Middle Easterners misidentified as Muslims) escalated after the terrorist attacks, and at least some of them were clearly motivated by patriolatry's fusion of piety and nationalism.

Moreover, big-ticket patriolaters, perhaps unintentionally but nonetheless irresponsibly, encouraged such outrages. Evangelist Franklin Graham, for example, publicly blasted Islam as a "wicked and evil" religion that "preaches violence." Televangelist Pat Robertson disagreed with Graham, but only because he denied that Islam is even a religion. Instead, he said, it's "a violent political system bent on the overthrow of governments of the world and world domination." Newt Gingerich further stirred the waters by announcing that building a proposed Islamic Center near New York City's ground zero was tantamount to Nazis putting up a billboard next to Washington DC's Holocaust Museum. Florida pastor Terry Jones blasted Islam and threatened to burn publicly as many Qur'ans as he could get his hands on in a patriolatrous auto de fe. Conservative pundits Paul Weyrich and William Lind condemned Islam as "quite simply a religion of war" and recommended the removal of Muslims from American soil.[9] This kind of rhetoric, frequently repeated and given generous media coverage, left its mark. By 2009, a full 70 percent of American Protestant clergy reported that they considered Islam a dangerous religion.[10] It's a safe bet that at least some of them shared their opinions with their congregations. One poll, for example,

---

[9] For these quotations, see Philip Jenkins, "Dark Passages," *The Boston Globe* (March 8, 2009).

[10] Adele M. Banks, "Survey: Two-Thirds of Protestant Pastors Consider Islam 'Dangerous,'" *USA Today* (December 21, 2009).

revealed that a full 11 percent of churchgoers were urged from the pulpit in 2004 to vote for the presidential candidate who could best protect the country from Muslim terrorists.[11]

This righteously indignant division of the world into "us" and "them" raises one of Patriot god idolatry's most frightening possibilities: *armed* crusadism, not just the Restoring Honor Rally kind. Crusaders always believe that their cause is just because holy. They see their struggles as apocalyptic ones between good and evil. Recall, for example, the holy-war rhetoric used by some American and British supporters of the 2002 Second Gulf War. Because there's no room for ambivalence about who the good (us) and bad (them) guys are, American patriolaters believe that their deity has granted the United States wide latitude in the tactics and weapons it can employ against foreign enemies. At its crudest level this way of thinking encourages individual acts of violence such as those perpetrated against random American Muslims. At its most epic, it leads to warfare for the sake of American and, so far as patriolaters are concerned, biblical ideals such as freedom, democracy, and free enterprise. Patriot-god followers tend to be strong boosters of military expansionism. At the outbreak of the Second Gulf War, nearly 70 percent of Protestant evangelicals supported the invasion.[12] Though public opinion, including theirs, has since soured on armed US involvement in the Middle East, evangelicals still defend a strong American military presence throughout the world. It's no coincidence that military chaplains are overwhelmingly drawn from the Protestant evangelical tradition.[13]

The crusader mentality can encourage and in turn be energized by what Walter Wink and other theologians call the

---

[11] Bill McKibben, "The Christian Paradox: How a Faith Nation Gets Jesus Wrong," *Harpers* (August 2005).

[12] Jim Lobe, "Conservative Christians Biggest Backers of Iraq War," *Common Dreams* (October 10, 2002).

[13] Tim Townsend, "Evangelical Christianity Disproportionately Represented by Military Chaplains," *Huffington Report* (January 12, 2011).

myth of redemptive violence.[14] This way of thinking maintains that violence, if performed in the service of God, is actually redemptive rather than wicked, and accordingly pleases God. The point is that some evils—perpetrated, of course, by "them"—are so dastardly that they can only be washed away by blood. This is music to the ear of a patriolater who at one and the same time feels himself encircled by enemies and called by both country and his god to battle the forces of wickedness. His chronic anxiety, when blended with the confidence that his nation has been handpicked for divine favor, is a volatile mixture.

A fundamental inconsistency

Bill McKibben, the environmentalist and social commentator who also, by the way, is one of those liberal Christians despised by Glenn Beck, once claimed that "America is simultaneously the most professedly Christian of the developed nations and the least Christian in its behavior."[15] This may be too harsh an indictment, but it can scarcely be denied that there's some truth to it. The discrepancy between profession and behavior that McKibben targets arises in part from the inherent inconsistency of patriolatry. In their attempt to fuse American nationalism and Christianity, worshipers of Patriot god struggle to cram square pegs into round holes.

The problem isn't that patriolaters invoke the gospel as a yardstick by which to measure social, economic, and political policies. The problem is that they *don't*. Their religious vision is informed first and foremost by an *über*-America

---

[14] The best short discussion of the myth of redemptive violence is found in Walter Wink, *Jesus and Nonviolence: A Third Way* (Minneapolis, MN: Augsburg Press, 2003). More ambitious readers might want to read his *The Powers That Be: Theology for a New Millennium* (New York: Doubleday, 1998). Several interesting videos of Wink speaking about the myth are available on YouTube.

[15] McKibben, "The Christian Paradox."

nationalism—"my country, right or wrong"—to which their particular spin on scripture and Christianity serves as handmaiden. Put another way, American devotees of Patriot god put their religion in the service of a recognizably conservative partisan political and social agenda. It's not that they first scour the scriptures to discern what Jesus wants them to do. More often than not, their partisanship forcibly seizes Jesus and leads him where he would not wish to go. This is McKibben's point, and it ought to be taken seriously.

Look at what characterizes Patriot god. He likes to favor one country and its inhabitants over all others. So, on the one hand, his love is selective; on the other hand, it's also indiscriminate, because as it turns out, anything his favored nation does to protect itself or extend its power is fine by him. He apparently favors the competition and rugged individualism associated with the American ideal of free enterprise, endorses the stockpiling of weapons (including ones of mass destruction), and the buildup of the military, and is more concerned about sexual mores than about social injustice or economic inequality. He favors conservative politicians and disapproves of liberal ones, stamps a seal of approval on big business but deplores big government, wants prayer in public school and the Ten Commandments on courthouse walls, blesses capital punishment but curses abortion, and is a solid supporter of a citizen's right to bear arms.

Yet as McKibben and others point out, none of what pleases Patriot god can be found in the New Testament, even though American patriolaters insist that their nation's values are founded on biblical ones. Both the letter and the spirit of what Jesus taught points to a God who loves profligately. In Christ there is no Jew or Gentile, man or woman, free or enslaved. Jesus commands us to love our neighbors in the same way, regardless of how foreign they seem to us. Jesus's God privileges the marginalized and disreputable over the powerful and established; warns against striving for worldly success, wealth, and power at the neglect of simplicity and humility;

abhors violence and recommends turning the other cheek rather than responsively, much less preemptively, striking; and teaches that primary allegiance should be to the kingdom of God, which is open to all, rather than to a political empire that sharply distinguishes "them" from "us." In short, if Patriot-god devotees really took scripture as seriously as they claim to, their vision of America would be quite different than it is. This is the inconsistency that lies at the heart of their idolatry and that McKibben calls them on.

The worm at the heart of American Patriot-god worship is its partisanship. It distorts the gospel's universally applicable message by tying it exclusively to a historically specific vision of American exceptionalism. Unlike the social teachings of papal encyclicals or the deep biblical roots of the civil rights movement, patriolatry concerns itself with nationalistic apologetics. Its god is one of power, not love. A sharp-eyed and steel-taloned American eagle, not a scourged man hanging from a cross who died for everyone, is its most appropriate religious symbol. Despite its reliance on biblical language, the creed of Patriot-god worship is incompatible with the Christianity it claims for itself.

The Bible is pretty clear that religion works best when it steers clear of partisan political alliances. Time and again in both the Old and New Testaments, we see God-sanctioned challenges to the existing political and social order. Moses defies mighty Pharaoh, the prophets speak out against kings who abuse power and the morally corrupt rich, Daniel and the three Hebrew youths stand up to Nebuchadnezzar, and Jesus challenges the power and greed upon which temple and state were (and often still are) built. The biblical message couldn't be more clear: the promise of redemptive freedom offered by God can't be written into any political or social blueprint that legitimizes nationalistic exceptionalism and the exclusionism, intolerance, militarism, and faux-religious symbolism that goes with it. Whatever else the version of Christianity spun by patriolaters may be, it's not one preached by

Jesus, who explicitly rejected dividing people into sheep and goats solely on the basis of something as accidental as their place of birth. He knew that there is a deeper loyalty than to one's country. As the Psalmist pithily noted (10:16), nations come and nations go, but God reigns forever.

Chapter 5

We Can Do It! god

*"Martha, Martha, you are worried
and distracted by many things; there
is need of only one thing."*
— LUKE 10:41–42

*The political task of Christians is to
be the church rather than to transform the world.*
— STANLEY HAUERWAS AND
WILLIAM H. WILLIMON[1]

For thirty years it's been one of the most recognizable posters
in the United States: the 1942 vintage portrait of Rosie the
Riveter, a determined-faced woman who flexes her arm at a
ninety-degree angle to make a muscle while proudly proclaim-
ing: *"We can do it!"* The poster first appeared in the middle of
World War II to boost the morale of women who filled factory
jobs left behind by their soldier husbands, fathers, brothers,
and boyfriends. It was rediscovered a generation later, and the
bandana-wearing Rosie became a popular icon.

---

[1] Stanley Hauerwas and William H. Willimon, *Resident Aliens* (Nash-
ville, TN: Abingdon Press, 1989), 38.

Rosie's stalwart confidence that *we can do it!* is a pep talk all of us occasionally need. Students benefit from hearing it from teachers, athletes from coaches, patients from physicians, children from parents, and spouses from each other. Folks working together for some political or social cause, whether economic reform or peace with justice, need to believe that their efforts are making a difference, even—*especially*—if the odds seem stacked against them. And who among us hasn't profited from our inner voice urging us on—*c'mon, you can do it!*—when our bodies ached and our spirits lagged and all we wanted to do was give up and lie down?

Rosie's determination is clearly admirable on one level. But like all good intentions, it can pave the road to hell when it mutates. Most obviously, it can fuel horribly wicked deeds and programs: apartheid, ponzi schemes, political corruption, ethnic cleansing, terrorist attacks. Career criminals, whether breaking the law or acting as "legitimate" members of political, religious, or social organizations, certainly steel themselves to achieve their ends through hard work and perseverance. In their hands, *we can do it!* becomes a demonic battle cry.

Rosie's way of thinking can also give rise to the worship of an idol called We Can Do It! god. In some ways this is perhaps the most benign of all the idolatries examined in this book, or at least the one that seems the least obviously destructive. It's often difficult to discern where legitimate service to the living God ends and obeisance to We Can Do It! god begins. Devotees of both see striving to make the world a better place to live as a cardinal obligation. Both take seriously Jesus's special concern for the poor, the sick, and the socially marginalized; his recommendation of the works of mercy and justice; the early Christian community's devotion to helping widows and orphans; and the two-thousand-year history (albeit one with rough spots) of Christian teaching on social justice.

But here's the distinction: We Can Do It! god–devotees see their deity as a divine coach whose main concern and primary job is rallying the team to repair a broken world. Can Doers believe that the *only* way of honoring their god is in *continuously* engaging in good works, even at the sacrifice of quiet, solitude, and prayer? Their religious life revolves around membership in dozens of parish committees, civic organizations, and political action groups. They maintain that the church's god-ordained role is to be a social service provider and a political lobbyist. They're constantly in motion, always on the go, forever throwing themselves body and soul into one cause or another, until eventually they lose the ability to be still and know God. When I think of a Can Doer—and I confess to having strong tendencies in that direction myself—the image that immediately comes to mind is the Tasmanian Devil in the old Warner Brothers cartoon. Remember him? He moves so swiftly that he looks like a mini-whirlwind, whipping up sandstorms in his path. He gets from point A to point B fast, but it's not clear that he accomplishes much of anything except a change of location, and by the time he gets where he's going, he's tongue-drooping-out-of-mouth exhausted. That's an image worth keeping in mind. Even when Can Doers' efforts are fruitful for others, their whirlwind-like service to their god ultimately leaves them physically exhausted, emotionally drained, and spiritually dry.

Idle hands

In one of the most influential sociological studies of religion ever written, *The Protestant Ethic and the Spirit of Capitalism*, Max Weber argued that citizens in capitalist societies are so fixated on productivity that they live to work rather than the other way around and that they actually feel morally diminished when unable to work. He believed that this work ethos was inseparably interwoven with the rise of Northern European Protestantism. His theory was that the Reformation ethos substituted worldly success for papal blessing as the mark of divine approval. As reliance on priestly assurances of salvation diminished, confidence grew that hard work was pleasing to God—an assumption that conveniently bestowed theological legitimacy on budding capitalist ambitions. The notion that idle hands are the devil's tools became both a religious principle and an economic maxim.

Can Doers are the spiritual heirs of this ethos. But they differ in one crucial respect from early Reformers. Instead of interpreting personal worldly success as a mark of divine favor, the success they aim for is improvement of the world. This is what pleases We Can Do It! god—in fact, it's why he created humans—and anything else takes second place. What he really values is for a devotee to roll up her sleeves, flex her muscles, and tackle anything that stands in the way of progress. Corporate worship, theological doctrine, private devotions: these are all negotiable. The commandment to turn idle hands into helping ones isn't. We Can Do It! god expects—*demands*—that his followers become lifelong reformers, social workers, and do-gooders. Their job is to come through for the divine Gipper.

On the surface it's hard to fault this passion for improving the world. God knows that it needs all the help it can get. We're all familiar with the sorry facts, or at least we ought to be. Over three billion people, half of the world's population, live on less than three dollars a day. Eighteen children die each and every minute of the day and night from poverty-related illnesses. Some forty armed conflicts are currently being fought around the world, not counting drug wars. Many of them are waged by child soldiers, kids who have been kidnapped, brutalized, and brainwashed into becoming stone-cold killers. Political repression, ethnic discrimination, and religious persecution continue to destroy human lives around the globe. And on top of all that, anthropogenic environmental degradation, global warming, and extreme weather patterns are reaching the point of no return, further aggravating tensions within and among nations.

In other words, the world's a mess, and millions of people are suffering. If there was ever a time for Rosie the Riveter determination, surely it's now. So how can wanting to do good be a form of idolatry?

The obvious answer is that wanting to help in and of itself *isn't* idolatrous. But devotees of We Can Do It! god place such a high premium on good works that everything else in the spiritual life gets shoved to the back of the line. Religion becomes a matter of morality and civic mindedness. God becomes a political and social campaign manager who hands out field assignments to devotees. Their spiritual goal is to cover as much territory as they can, and it leaves them no time or energy for cultivating much of an interior life. Their busy days are too crammed from dawn to dark with committee meetings, interviews, fund raising, troubleshooting, working soup lines, distributing clothes, meeting with legislators, and occasionally marching in the streets to allow quiet moments of prayerful recollection. But that's OK, because We Can Do It! god doesn't put much stock in such things anyway—at least not while a devotee is able-bodied enough to work. There'll be time enough for meditation and prayer when the world has been made a better place to live in, or when age or illness takes a devotee out of the field. For Can Doers, work is their way of praying, and that's precisely the sort of prayer their god wants. Hands should be in motion, not clasped.

No one can deny that Can Doers actually get a lot of good done. They build schools, bring water to thirsty villages, establish homeless shelters, and help to keep politicians (not to mention ecclesial authorities) honest. But their way of thinking also inspired the muscular European Christianity of bygone centuries that sent thousands of white missionaries to bring salvation to benighted "heathens" in America, Africa, and Asia. Along the way, of course, their "civilizing" regimens frequently disrupted local communities and destroyed traditional ways of life, all for the greater glory of Can Do god. The heyday of religious colonialism has thankfully passed. But the good intentions of Can Doers can still cause damage. Today, many of them serve their deity by organizing powerful political action committees and lobbying for public policy reform. But to reach their spiritual bottom line, they often must embrace tactics and enter into collaborations that are morally questionable and spiritually corrosive. Because their ultimate standard of spiritual success is outcome based, Can Doers can find themselves forced to "dine with the devil." Still, they conclude, better to take one step backward for the sake of two steps forward than to remain immobile.

What is it that drives Can Doers into the arms of their god? As with all idolaters, fear plays an important role. What they most fear is not being effective agents in the world, not being powerful enough to get things done, being seen by themselves and others—and, most crucially, by their god—as passive or impotent. Can Doers are able to tolerate the occasional failure—after all, not every hungry child can be fed, or every polluted river cleaned up—but what they can't stomach is inactivity, either their own or anyone else's. They—*we*—were put on this earth to do, not to sit about idly. A human is measured by how stalwartly he puts his shoulder to the grindstone, how loyally he soldiers on even when the odds are stacked against him, and how successful he is in doing We Can Do It! god's work.

It should be kept in mind that Can Doers' fear of impotence could just as easily have turned their energies to the pursuit of personal gain and power. Instead, they chose to use their skills and expend their energy to help others achieve better lives. Their natural inclinations push them in the direction of service rather than selfishness. Their hearts are large enough for compassion, and that draws them closer to the living God than any other kind of idolater discussed in this book. But their compassion, while an important indicator of their character, is secondary to their dread of idle hands and their panic at the thought of impotence. And that suggests that under the wrong conditions, it can give way to recrimination and self-righteousness. Can Doers are always at risk of sliding into Big Brotherism.

Can Doer heresy

Max Weber explained how Protestantism and capitalism merged to create an ethos in which spiritual success came to be measured in terms of outcome-based standards. A generation after Weber his fellow countryman Josef Pieper shed light on the spiritual peril facing a culture that fixates on work at the expense of leisure or relaxation. His analysis goes a long way toward explaining how We Can Do It! idolatry damages its followers.[2]

Pieper argued that a culture obsessed with work, regardless of whether it's for personal profit or in the service of humanity, is one that also overvalues control. A worker, even one engaged in physical drudgery, exerts power, even if the power is no more significant than "commanding" a spadeful of earth to relocate from here to there. The relative place of the work in the social pecking order isn't the bottom-line standard of evaluation. Activity, exertion of power, is. Workers actively perform rather than passively receive; they are the givers rather than the recipients. They make things happen, thereby asserting authority and creating identities for themselves. So long as they remain active, busy, on-the-job, they possess some degree of control or command and so have some degree of value. Once out of a job, no longer productive, functionless, they become disempowered losers, useless and expendable.

Now, a work-fixated culture obviously gets things done. The trains run on time, and factories churn out widgets. But Pieper worried that the obsession with work—with always being productively busy—comes with a high price tag. For starters, it erodes our ability to relax in the conventional sense of the word. Remember the wonderful movie *Modern Times*, in which Charlie Chaplin plays a factory worker

---

[2] Pieper criticizes what he calls a "total-work" society in a magnificent little book entitled *Leisure: The Basis of Culture* (New York: Pantheon, 1952).

unable to stop his hands from making assembly line motions even after the work day ends? Are we really all that different today? Americans work longer hours than people in any other industrialized nation, including Japan. Many of us hold down more than one job, and those of us who don't often feel as if we're always on call. Our BlackBerry stays on even when we're off the clock, we put in extra hours at the end of the day and on the weekends, and an increasing number of us find it difficult to enjoy ourselves during vacation time for thinking about work. We just don't know what to do with ourselves when we're not "productively" busy. To help get through our holidays, we often choreograph them with comfortingly hectic schedules ("if this is Tuesday, it must be Belgium"), or throw ourselves into having "fun" in noisy and frenetic ways that are anything but relaxing. Even then, we're likely to fret and fidget until we can get back to the job. Our exaggerated valuation of work leads us to feel uneasy with ourselves when we're inactive, even when on holiday or vacation, because we've been taught to associate sloth, laziness, or impotence with inactivity, and power and dignity with busyness.

As if this isn't bad enough, a work-fixated culture inhibits our ability to relax in a spiritual sense as well. *Relax* comes from a Latin word meaning "to open," "to loosen," or "to make something less dense or compact." ("You need to loosen up!" we tell a tightly-wound person.) Pieper thinks this etymology is significant, because from a religious perspective it suggests calming down long enough to open oneself to the presence of God. This, in turn, suggests that what a work-fixated culture dismisses as sloth or idleness may, under certain circumstances, be a necessary condition for genuine spiritual growth. In making his case Pieper appeals both to Aristotle, who insisted that work is valuable not in itself but because its fruits buy us the time to relax, and to Thomas Aquinas, who insightfully argued that sloth isn't inactivity so much as a restless inability to relax.

It's not hard to see why relaxation is so important when it comes to the spiritual life. When we relax, we let go of the need to be in control of things. Instead of tensely sizing up situations to see what opportunities they offer for seizure and manipulation—a work- and power-obsessed mode of comportment—we make ourselves "less dense or compact." Suspending our urges to clutch and dominate, we allow ourselves simply to experience. It's as if we become what Ralph Waldo Emerson once strikingly called a "transparent eyeball," an act of pure perception that gazes upon the world without any external or internal impediment. Zen Buddhists compare this state of utter receptivity with a spotlessly clean pane of glass through which sunlight passes without blemish or distortion.

The alert attentiveness gestured at by both Emerson and the Zen tradition is a radical openness not only to the world but also, from a religious perspective, to God. Human reason, imagination, and discourse always fall short in the face of divine plenitude. But this doesn't mean that humans are incapable of spontaneous experiences of God that, although eluding clear-cut analysis or description, are both revelatory and transformative. Mystics from all traditions testify to their reality. But these experiences come, if at all, only when a quiet, still, and uncluttered space has been cleared within the soul to make room for them. Only then is wisdom and insight possible.

Can Doers don't get this. For them, inactivity or relaxation isn't just morally culpable laziness; with all the world's problems that cry out for attention, it's also sinful heresy. Taking the time to cultivate quiet receptivity strikes them as self-indulgence masquerading as spirituality, and they're not averse to letting it be known that truly devout folks oughtn't to allow themselves such luxuries. Years ago I found myself volunteering in a church kitchen on Thanksgiving Day. Clients had been congregating outside all morning, and things promised to get hectic on the serving line once the meal started. Just before the doors were thrown open to let the crowds rush in, one of my fellow volunteers, perhaps apprehensive about the tidal wave about to hit, blurted out, "Shouldn't we say a prayer or something before we begin?" The kitchen director, a long-time advocate for the homeless, impatiently snapped: "We don't have time to pray. There's too much to be done!" I'm not saying the director was a Can Doer, but what she said is a perfect example of the Can Do spirit.

Here's another example, from one of the best television shows to come down the pike in ages. The BBC comedy *Rev* follows the misadventures of a sweet but bumbling Father Adam Smallbone, an Anglican priest in an inner-city London parish. In one episode Adam is on quiet retreat at a monastery, grateful for a break from his busy schedule. By coincidence, one of his old school chums, a flashy celebrity priest who's always on the go, turns up at the same monastery for *his* retreat. But, predictably, cloistered silence doesn't fit him at all well. He paces restlessly up and down in his small cell until, unable to take it any longer, he strides over to the window, throws it open, and bellows out a Can Doer protest. "We shouldn't be doing this here, though, should we?" he yells. "We should be out there, in the community, making our marks, telling the word: telly, radio, twitter, the lot! The church just doesn't get front-foot enough! Too much praying! Not enough action!" Monastic silence? Contemplative quietude? Heresy!

Given their conviction that the best way to worship their deity is by bustling to save the world, it's not surprising that Can Doers suffer from a cumulative weariness that can lead to episodic or permanent burnout. Social service and relief work is draining, especially if one empathizes deeply, as Can Doers genuinely do, with the suffering of the people one wants to help. To sustain psychological and physical (not to mention spiritual) health, people who dedicate themselves to the service of others require periodic down time from work in which to relax and recharge their batteries. But as we've seen, workaholics in general do badly with down time, and Can Doers are generally too busy serving their god to cultivate much of an interior life. So the risk of depression, despair, and burnout is high for them. Even worse, when burnout comes, they believe they've failed their god, since what he requires of them is unflagging service to the world. After all, the depressive paralysis that accompanies burnout is a form of passivity, and in a world that needs saving, passivity is sinful.

There's another cause of Can Doer burnout, and it goes back to outcome-based standards. We saw earlier that devotees of We Can Do It! god can tolerate a certain amount of failure just so long as they see themselves conscientiously striving to do the good their deity demands. But because success is so important to them, and because even the most dedicated and tireless effort on their part won't save the world, the cumulative effect of plugging hole after hole in a never-endingly leaky dike can be devastating.

The pit into which Can Doers fall is the presumption that their efforts fall short of what their tireless god demands unless they can stop *all* the leaks. No credit's given for partial success. The only acceptable outcome is complete success. It's as simple as that. Can Doers don't realize that work undertaken for God is properly measured by a different standard of success. Spiritual leaders from all traditions have always taught that religiously inspired activists should keep their attention focused on the task at hand—washing an ill person, feeding someone who's hungry, or simply holding the hand of a dying person—and not allow themselves to be distracted over concerns about outcome. The point is to be single-mindedly present to the person being served rather than to fragment attention and energy by fretting over the odds of failure or success. To do God's work is to give oneself fully and lovingly to another. That's sufficient in itself. This is a hard lesson to learn for those of us who have Can Do tendencies, much less for dedicated Can Doers.

Being the church

If that's the case, how can one go about serving others without falling into Can Doerism? What does it mean to focus on the task at hand instead of keeping an eye on the prize? What might this kind of service, one that strikes an outcomes-obsessed culture as utterly fey, look like in practice?

American theologians Stanley Hauerwas and William Willimon have a suggestion. They worry that mainstream American denominations embrace secular society's standard of busyness as their own in the hope of seeming relevant to a culture that's increasingly unenthusiastic about the Christian message. The upshot, they contend, is that "what we call 'church' is too often a gathering of strangers who see the church as yet another 'helping institution' to gratify further their individual desires"—in this case, the Can Do urge to save the world. Churches are in danger of trading in their unique religious identities for the sake of becoming social service agencies. They are drifting toward an emphasis on civic commitment and away from Christian proclamation. Their methods are no longer "preaching, baptism, and witness to form a visible community of faith," but rather the manipulation of secular tools to bend public policy. Consequently, Christians today are increasingly "content" with "lobbying Congress to support progressive strategies, asking the culture at large to be a little less racist, a little less promiscuous, a little less violent." The effectiveness of the lobbying is what ultimately counts, because lobbying always keeps its eye on the prize: success, power, getting the job done.[3]

Now, Hauerwas and Willimon aren't arguing that churches ought not to speak truth to power or come to the aid of people in trouble. Instead, their point is that when churches begin to think of themselves as social agencies and strive to accommodate themselves to the secular political process, they risk losing their core identities and falling under the spell of We Can Do It! god. They're in danger of forgetting that they're colonies of resident aliens who live in but are not of the world. Using Pauline language, Hauerwas and Willimon insist that Christians are "ambassadors of Christ" rather than

---

[3] Hauerwas and Willimon, *Resident Aliens,* 138, 80.

citizens of a work-fixated society. Their proper community embodies an ethos that "the world cannot on its own terms know."[4]

Read one way, Hauerwas and Willimon might seem to be recommending a separatist policy of withdrawal, with churches keeping their distance from the rest of the world by retreating into segregated enclaves. This isn't a totally unreasonable interpretation, especially since Hauerwas is extremely influenced by the Anabaptist tradition. But he and Willimon aren't advocating retreat *from* the world so much as encouraging Christians to affirm their identity *to* the world. Churches help people and influence public policy in a way that's unique to them: they witness, in word and deed, to the God of love, even to the point of sacrificing wealth, reputation, social power, and sometimes life. They testify to the truth that busyness in a secular context oughtn't to be the highest value, and that busyness in the service of God is downright misguided because it gets in the way of cultivating the interior loving relationship with God that, above all, defines Christians and constitutes their greatest gift to the world. Given this, the business of the church is simply to *be church,* to exemplify the gospel for the rest of humankind by demonstrating "that God, not nations, rules the world, that the boundaries of God's kingdom transcend those of Caesar, and that the main political task of the church is the formation of people who see clearly the cost of discipleship and are willing to pay the price."[5]

What's going on here is a radical reaffirmation of Christian living. A Christian's priority must always be loving discipleship to the living God, and such discipleship requires a progressive opening up of the soul and mind to the presence of God. As we've seen, this is possible only when the disciple intentionally makes room in his life for periods of "relaxation" that tutor him in how to listen for and to God.

---

[4] Ibid., 18.
[5] Ibid., 48.

The more he listens in silence and humility, the stronger the loving relationship between him and God grows.

So the Christian's priority, unlike the Can Doer's, is most definitely *not* to fix the world. But here's the thing: by remaining loyal to his identity as a resident alien, the Christian inevitably practices love of neighbors. Moreover, his example is so startlingly countercultural that the rest of the world takes notice. "See how these Christians love one another—and us!" So much good in and for the world is done not by the busily self-defeating worship of We Can Do It! god, which aims to fix the world first and to love second, but by loving God first and foremost and thereby being empowered in the truest sense of the word to serve a suffering world. As Jesus gently told Martha, the godmother of all Can Doers, only one thing is really needed. Then everything else falls into place.

Chapter 6

By the Book god

> The Bible is the inerrant . . . word of
> the living God. It is absolutely infal-
> lible, without error in all matters per-
> taining to faith and practice, as well
> as in areas such as geography, science,
> history, etc.
>
> —JERRY FALWELL

> Sad, indeed, would the whole matter
> be, if the Bible had told us everything
> God meant us to believe. But herein is
> the Bible itself greatly wronged. It no-
> where lays claim to be regarded as the
> Word, the Way, the Truth. The Bible
> leads us to Jesus, the inexhaustible,
> the ever unfolding Revelation of God.
>
> —GEORGE MACDONALD[1]

Nearly half a century ago Alvin Toffler coined the term
"future shock" to refer to what he saw as an affliction of

---

[1] Jerry Falwell, *Finding Inner Peace and Strength* (New York: Doubleday, 1982), 126, 127; George MacDonald, *Unspoken Sermons, Series
One* (London: Longmans, Green, and Co, 1867), 36.

the modern information age. Future shock is "the shattering stress and disorientation" induced in us when we're subjected to "too much change in too short a time."[2] We simply can't keep psychological pace with the avalanche of novel ideas, technologies, facts, and norms constantly hurtling toward us, and our coping techniques range from a bewildered shutting down to an angry suspicion of anything new. Toffler wrote in the early days of the computer age. Future shock was a problem even then. The breathlessly rapid turnover of information made possible by today's Internet has only aggravated it.

Actually, the malady had been around for years before Toffler put a name to it. Whenever new learning appeared on the scene so suddenly that people had trouble adjusting to it, future shock–like symptoms were distinct possibilities. European and North American Christians began to feel them in the eighteenth century when Enlightenment-inspired "higher biblical criticism"—the discipline of rigorously analyzing scripture as historical and literary texts—became an increasingly prominent feature of the religious landscape. Many Christians were shocked by what they took to be the impious challenge to biblical authority posed by the higher criticism and drew a line in the sand by insisting that the only proper way to read the Bible was to accept it as inerrant—factually accurate and logically consistent in every respect. A proper Christian, they insisted, should accept the Bible as the literal word of God and embrace every proposition contained within it as "gospel truth."

As anyone living in the United States surely knows, belief in biblical inerrancy is alive and well today. A 2011 Gallup poll revealed that 30 percent of Christians believe scripture to be "the actual word of God, and is to be taken literally, word for word."[3] For them, the last two centuries of textual criticism are irrelevant at best, blasphemous at worst. The same goes

---

[2] Alvin Toffler, *Future Shock* (New York: Bantam, 1984), 2.
[3] Jeffrey M. Jones, "In US, 3 in 10 Say They Take the Bible Literally," *Gallup* (July 8, 2011).

for the last two centuries of science. What *is* relevant to them is the fundamentalist slogan: The Bible says it, I believe it, that settles it! It's the philosophy they live and die by.

But what they live and die by is bibliolatrous, because they've embraced as their ultimate concern a book rather than God. They worship a By the Book god made of paper, ink, and (at least in the more expensive editions) leather. Overwhelmed by a future shock that threatens their safe religious world, they burrow deeply into the Book, stuff their ears with its pages to drown out anything they don't want to hear, and endlessly chew on its words, often memorizing but rarely thinking about them. ("Let anyone with ears listen!") They invest the actual words with an absolute authority that justifies using them as bludgeons against whomever they condemn as an infidel—namely, anyone, Christian or otherwise, who doesn't accept the inerrancy of scripture. Reading scripture, By the Bookers believe, is the same as standing in the presence of God and hearing his voice. Defending the Bible down to its very last jot and tittle is their primary religious duty.

Why bibliolatry is mistaken

A particularly good summary of the bibliolatry practiced by By the Bookers is the 1978 Chicago Statement on Biblical Inerrancy. The result of a decade-long study conducted by several hundred evangelicals for the International Council on Biblical Inerrancy, the document is a convenient everything-you-need-to-know catechism for devotees of By the Book god. Two of its claims are foundational.[4]

First, the Chicago Statement on Biblical Inerrancy makes it clear that when it comes to the Bible, the approach is all or nothing. "The authority of Scripture is inescapably impaired if this total divine inerrancy is in any way limited or disregarded." This is because "Scripture in its entirety is inerrant,

---

[4]The full text of the Chicago Statement on Biblical Inerrancy is available on the www.reformed.org website.

being free from all falsehood, fraud, or deceit" (Article 13). Second, according to the statement, not only must every word from Genesis to Revelation be accepted as absolutely true, but the Bible is also the final arbiter in *all* areas of human investigation and knowledge. "We deny that Biblical infallibility and inerrancy are limited to spiritual, religious, or redemptive themes, exclusive of assertions in the fields of history and science" (Article 12).

In short, the statement affirms the notion that the Bible is not only the sole source of knowledge about God, moral norms, and daily living—everything that falls into the categories of faith and religious practice—but also of history, science, cosmology, politics, aesthetics, medicine, and any other field of human inquiry one might care to mention. So, it turns out that the Bible is omniscient—and omniscience, of course, is a divine attribute. Moreover, because it's totally free of error, the Bible is also perfect—another divine quality. Additionally, the Bible is supernatural because it's the *revealed* word of God. And to cap everything off, the Bible is redemptive, because it contains everything necessary for human salvation. There you have it: God in a Book.

Now, if you accuse a By the Book-god devotee of bibliolatry, she will hotly deny the charge. She'll point out that she doesn't bow down before the Bible or place it on an altar surrounded by candles or offer sacrifices to it. She doesn't pray to it or express gratitude to it. She doesn't even see it as a holy relic. It is, she will insist, a path to God, not itself a god.

But it's not out of line here to invoke the "if it looks like a duck, walks like a duck, and quacks like a duck" rule of thumb. From a functional perspective, the By the Booker endows the Bible with godlike qualities, places absolute trust in it, refuses to countenance any questioning of it, consults it for advice, consolation, and insight, and accepts it as the final arbiter in interpersonal as well as intellectual disputes. Just as astonishingly, a By the Booker argues that the Bible is self-sufficient, self-justifying, self-legitimizing—exactly what you'd expect a deity to be. The Good Book's self-validation is proclaimed in Article XV of the Chicago Statement: "The doctrine of inerrancy is grounded in the teaching of the Bible about inspiration." What does this mean?

According to this By the Book doctrine, a perfectly sufficient justification for accepting the Bible as the inerrant word of God is because the Bible says it is. Bibliolaters appeal to a handful of proof texts to make their case. Some of the ones most frequently cited include the following: "The promises of the Lord are promises that are pure" (Ps 12:6); "All scripture is inspired by God,[5] and is useful for teaching, for reproof, for correction, and for training in righteousness" (2 Tim 3:16–17); and "no prophecy of scripture is a matter of one's own interpretation, because no prophecy ever came by human will, but men and women moved by the Holy Spirit spoke from God" (2 Pet 1:20–21).

Obviously, if one accepts the inerrancy of scripture, it follows that these passages must be accepted as absolutely true. But for anyone other than a By the Booker, there's an obvious and troublesome circularity at play here: invoking bible verses as evidence for the inerrancy of scripture is persuasive only if one's already accepted the inerrancy of scripture. Bibliolaters respond by dismissing this as faithless hairsplitting. But despite their protests, this kind of circularity hoists the warning flag pretty high. Sacred texts from many other religious traditions also claim to be "God breathed." Merely saying so establishes nothing.

Another red flag that bibliolatry raises is the inference from 2 Peter that scripture (or at least prophecy) should be read without interpretation. But it's not at all clear what this means. When it comes to reading anything, including works as prosaic as instruction manuals and cook books, interpretation seems to be normative. The likelihood of interpretively reading a book like the Bible is so high that it classifies as inevitable. Over the centuries exegetes have defended multiple and sometimes wildly divergent readings of the same texts. Part of the reason

---

[5] The Greek beautifully reads "God-breathed."

for the breadth of biblical interpretation stems from the fact that many scriptural passages claiming to be historical or empirical descriptions defy ordinary human experience, contradict one another, or simply make no sense. The rise of biblical criticism was, in fact, a reaction to these and other difficulties that emerge if one tries to read the scriptures literally.

Bibliolaters generally try to get around the objection that scripture often seems meaningless or false in the absence of interpretation with a "nevertheless!" kind of argument. The Chicago Statement on Biblical Inerrancy, for example, denies (without offering an explanation) that biblical inerrancy is negated by the text's "lack of modern technical precision, irregularities of grammar or spelling, observational descriptions of nature, the reporting of falsehoods, the use of hyperbole and round numbers, the topical arrangement of material, variant selections of material in parallel accounts, or the use of free citations." Bizarrely, the statement goes on to insist that it's absolutely "improper" to evaluate the truth claims of the Bible "according to standards of truth and error that are alien to its usage or purpose" (Article 13). This slams the door shut on further discussion, because what it obviously means is that any statement that would properly raise eyebrows in a non-biblical text is somehow privileged when it's in the Bible. And what in the world would a standard of truth and error "alien" to the Bible be? Apparently one that refuses to accept as foundational the claim that the Bible as inerrant—taking us right back to the troublesome circularity that the Bible is inerrant because the Bible says it's inerrant.

Another By the Book dogma asserts that the doctrine of biblical inerrancy is as old as Christianity. In defending it, devotees say that they're simply returning to the purer, original way of reading scripture that was the norm before everything got corrupted by textual criticism. As the Chicago Statement on Biblical Inerrancy insists, the doctrine of inerrancy was neither invented by Protestantism nor is a reaction to "negative higher criticism," but instead "has been integral to the Church's faith throughout its history" (Article 16).

But the historical record is much more complex than that. As much as By the Bookers want to claim that their bibliolatry is really nothing more than a return to "that old time religion," the plain truth is that there's never been a united Christian front when it comes to the proper way to read scripture any more than there was one in the Judaism from which Christianity arose. At least as early as the fifth-century BCE Ezra, who "set his heart to study the law of the Lord" (Ezr 7:10), midrashic interpretation, aiming to uncover the deep meaning of sacred text, was the norm. By the beginning of the Middle Ages rabbinic exegetes worked under the assumption that there were actually four legitimate ways of interpreting scripture, abbreviated by the acronym PaRDeS ("paradise"). They were Peshat, a literal reading; Remez, a metaphorical reading; Derash, a reading that compares various midrashic interpretations; and Sod, a mystical reading. Nor did these modes of interpretation get in one another's way. Instead, they shed light on one another, revealing, in the rabbis' judgment, the richly interwoven layers of meaning embedded in biblical texts.

From a very early period Christian exegetes likewise disagreed about how to read scripture. In the late third century two rival schools of biblical exegesis emerged that set the tone for centuries to come. The Antiochian School focused primarily on a literal and historical reading of scripture, while the Alexandrian School defended an allegorical and mystical one. Paralleling the medieval emergence of the rabbinic PaRDeS method (the two probably cross-pollinated one another), Christian exegesis in the twelfth century adopted a fourfold approach to biblical interpretation. According to this model one perfectly appropriate although limited way was to read the Bible literally. But as one entered more deeply into the text, richer levels of meaning emerged: the typological or allegorical, the moral, and the anagogical or mystical. Like PaRDeS, this exegetical method saw no inconsistency in reading a single text through these four lenses because scripture itself is layered with meaning, some of it obvious, much of it arcane. To focus on one layer at the expense of the others isn't necessarily to misread the text, but it certainly is to *under*-read it.

So the By the Booker claim that scriptural inerrancy is the traditional exegetical assumption in the Christian tradition just isn't true. There certainly have been champions of inerrancy in every century of the Christian era. But they've never been the only players in the game, and in the modern era, contrary to the Chicago Statement on Biblical Inerrancy's assertion, inerrantists *are* reacting primarily to "negative higher criticism." Besides, even if it *were* historically true that earlier generations of Christians all tried to read the Bible literally, merely pointing that out wouldn't justify continuing to do so today. As one astute commentator puts it:

> The fact is that every human experience is interpreted by the experiencing person or it is not passed on. It is always interpreted within the framework by which that person comprehends what is real. When knowledge expands, it renders the interpretive framework of ancient people inadequate, and it reveals the ignorance of the past. For people living in one age to try to cling to the objective truthfulness of the concepts of another age is to participate in a doubtful enterprise.[6]

The pulse of bibliolatry

Given the irrationality of bibliolatry, what accounts for the fact that nearly one-third of Christians in the United States pay homage to By the Book god? His feet are so obviously made of clay that it's baffling he has any followers at all, much less such zealous ones. Although it's unpleasant to hear, one explanation goes a long way toward clearing up the puzzle.

Data suggest that many American By the Bookers know little more about the book they worship than what their

---

[6] John Shelby Spong, *Rescuing the Bible from Fundamentalism* (San Francisco: HarperSanFrancisco, 1991), 25.

bibliolatrous preachers choose to tell them in Sunday morning sermons. They aren't familiar with the history of exegesis; nor do they have firsthand acquaintance with the works of biblical scholars. If they know anything of higher criticism, it's likely because they've been warned away from it by their pastors. In short, many of By the Book god's devotees, for all their ability to quote chapter and verse on any occasion, are biblically illiterate. The same 2011 Gallup poll that discovered that 30 percent of US Christians are inerrantists also found that, the more educated Christians are, the less likely they are to be bibliolaters. Nearly 50 percent of Christians with a high school education or less said they believed that "the Bible is the actual word of God, and is to be taken literally, word for word." The percentage plummeted by over half with people who had some college, and dropped down to 15 percent for Christians who had graduated from college.[7]

What this suggests is that in the case of By the Bookers, future-shocked as they are by the avalanche of new information from biblical scholars, theologians, scientists, and non-Christian religious traditions that threatens their deepest convictions, ignorance becomes both a defensive shield and an offensive sword. Theologian Beverly Harrison puts her finger on the pulse of bibliolatry when she notes that it's motivated by an "insistence on a religious monopoly of knowledge grounded in fear of alternative knowledges, particularly 'scientific' modes of knowledge generated in modernity, which the 'God-knowledge' people cannot control."[8]

Challenged by alternative ways of explaining reality—ones, moreover, based on strong evidence and rigorous analysis— bibliolaters feel the ground being jerked out from under their feet. They also sense that the world is much more complex, and consequently less unambiguously black and white, than their religious comfort zone can accommodate. As Harrison

---

[7] Jones, "In US, 3 in 10 Say They Take the Bible Literally."

[8] Beverly Harrison, quoted in Daniel Maguire, *Sacred Choices* (Minneapolis, MN: Fortress Press, 2001), 123.

says, they feel their scripture-centered "religious monopoly of knowledge" challenged. Holding on to their worldview, reasserting their control, and escaping future shock depend on successful resistance to the challenge. So they plug their ears and shut their eyes. But this mode of resistance isn't much more than retrenchment. More aggressively, bibliolaters doggedly reaffirm the dogma of inerrancy by appealing again and again to favorite proof texts, loudly insisting on the primacy of biblical knowledge over all walks of human investigation and condemning any criticism of their position as grounded in standards of truth and error "alien" to the Bible.

Couple the high degree of biblical illiteracy with the fear-driven repudiation of "'scientific' modes of knowledge generated in modernity"—the sources of future shock—and it becomes clear that By the Bookers remain loyal to their idol only by cultivating willful ignorance.

We don't usually think of ignorance as a choice or matter of will, largely because we assume that garden-variety ignorance is the only kind there is, and it certainly doesn't imply any active decision on our part. On the contrary, it's a limitation of knowledge brought about by circumstance, with the usual assumption being that the limitation can be dissipated once we obtain more information. So, for example, I'm ignorant of what you, the reader, are wearing as you read these words. But it's not logically impossible (although it *is* highly improbable) for me somehow to find out (perhaps you're now being secretly skyped or photographed), thus replacing my ignorance with knowledge. Similarly, I'm ignorant about whether any other planets in the universe are inhabited. But that kind of ignorance is at least in principle fixable if we ever figure out how to travel into deep space. Garden variety ignorance is often more complicated than this, as when my knowledge is so constrained by circumstances that I'm actually ignorant of being ignorant of something. But even here, my double-dipped ignorance isn't willful. It's an honest absence of knowledge.

Willful ignorance, on the other hand, is a horse of an entirely different color. It *is* a choice, a deliberate refusal to examine anything that challenges our most cherished beliefs. It's not that circumstances constrain us from knowing the truth, but rather that we repudiate opportunities for doing so because we don't want our convictions, lifestyles, and outlooks ruffled. The well-known story of the Catholic prelates who refused even to look through Galileo's telescope lest their geocentrism be called into question is an illustration of willful ignorance, but so is the refusal of By the Bookers to consider the possibility that the mystery of God and the mind-boggling richness of God's creation aren't exhaustively trapped between the covers of a book.[9]

Mummification

Like all idolatries, worship of By the Book god both inhibits a genuine relationship with the living God and seriously damages the spiritual health of devotees. When God is imprisoned inside a book, a stale, motionless aridity replaces the invigorating wind of the Holy Spirit. A mummification takes place in which both the divine and the human become fixed in time—or perhaps I should say fixed *outside* of time.

Remember poor Miss Havisham from Charles Dickens's *Great Expectations?* She was jilted by her fiance at the very last minute, just as she was dressing for their wedding. Unable to cope with the abrupt change in her circumstances (her own tornado of future shock), she remains frozen in that exact moment for the rest of her life. She shuts up her house, receives no visitors, and continues wearing her wedding gown and the one shoe she had slipped on right before she received the bad news. She lives in perpetual twilight in an airless house full of decay, cobwebs, and dust. There is no future between its walls, and the present is nothing more than a ceaselessly looped replay of the past. For all practical purposes, Miss Havisham is a mummy and her house a tomb.

---

[9] For an illuminating discussion of willful ignorance, see James P. Carse, *The Religious Case Against Belief* (New York: Penguin, 2009).

Miss Havisham's fate is worth remembering here because it isn't all that different from the spiritual mummification that befalls bibliolaters. They too live in a house from which the future has been exiled and all that remains is a frozen present modeled on a largely mistaken notion of the past. Nothing stirs in their dwelling place. The furniture is never dusted, the attic never explored, the floors never swept, and the windows never opened. Time has stopped for them. They and their god have become static and one dimensional.

Why do I say this? Because the By the Book devotee denies that God still actively reveals himself in and to the world. The Chicago Statement on Biblical Inerrancy is explicit about this. "We deny that any normative revelation has been given since the completion of the New Testament writings" (Article 5). God has nothing new to say because everything worth saying was uttered two thousand years ago. At that particular point in time, apparently, divine vitality congealed, contracted, and confined itself forevermore within mostly black squiggles (some of them, the really important bits, are red) on the pages of a single book. God no longer speaks except through the squiggles, and so says the same thing over and over and over. He is a celestial mummy enthroned on an antiquated throne in an echo chamber. Art, new discoveries about the natural world, psychology, theology, philosophy, all fields of human inquiry, the beauty of nature, and the mystery of the stars will never be channels of divine communication. When it comes to God, all of creation except for a single book is silent. It *is* a curious inconsistency, though, that bibliolaters generally *do* allow for one type of ongoing revelation: the born-again experience.

But By the Book god isn't the only mummy. His devotees, made in the likeness of their deity, also live in a land in which time stands still and dust settles. Developing a genuine relationship with another, whether a fellow human or God, is a dynamic and living affair in which we get stretched, challenged, enlightened, and sometimes hurt by the interaction. In other words, meaningful relationships necessarily involve change, even when the change is painful. A relationship in which the partners shy away from change embalms them both in a static medium that stifles growth, even if it might, to some degree, insulate them from unpleasant truths. This stiflingly airless pseudo-relationship is the fate of those who worship By the Book god. It's not surprising that they end-lessly draw upon a reserve of stock verses when defending their bibliolatry. Nothing new gets added to their spiritual in-ventory, no growth is allowed, no future possibility explored, because they've internalized the shutdown nature of the god they worship.

Fingers and moons

I'm not much of a horror-film buff, but whenever I think of bibliolatry, a scene from the 1976 movie *The Omen* (the first and best one, starring Gregory Peck and Lee Remick) comes to mind. A priest, terrified by what he senses as the threaten-ing presence of demonic evil, lines every square inch of wall space in his apartment, even the windows, with pages torn from the Bible. He uses words as bricks to build a barrier against danger. As one of the film's characters rather need-lessly says when the room is discovered, "I think he was trying to keep something out."

Hiding behind his paper bulwark didn't protect the priest, who winds up meeting a particularly gruesome end despite all his precautions. But his fate was predictable, because he fun-damentally misunderstood what the Bible is. He mistook mere words about God for the living Word of God. He believed the words possessed a divine power that belongs to God alone. So in the end, his By the Book idol let him down—which, of course, it had to. Idols are anchors, not buoys.

Where the priest and other devotees of By the Book god go wrong is failing to see that the words in the Bible are signposts that point to something other than themselves. A bit of advice from the Zen tradition is appropriate here: When a wise person sees someone pointing at the moon, he knows that his attention is being directed toward the object pointed at, not toward the finger doing the pointing. By the Bookers confuse finger and moon. The words in the Bible struggle to express something that is inherently indescribable: the divine, all-encompassing, infinite Presence, the true Word of God. At best, they invoke and evoke. Like poetry, their message comes through both in what the words say and what they leave unsaid. To appreciate fully the story of God told in the Bible, we have to read the words but also meditate on the silent spaces between them. Doing so not only gestures at a fundamental truth about God—that all discourse about God falls far, far short of the reality—but also invites us to discern divine presence in all the silent spaces we encounter in our lives. Because if God is truly in our midst, God is in them too.

By the Book god is too crabbed, too mummified, and too wordy to be credible, and the spirituality his worship encourages is too unadventurous. God is *not* the Bible. Sometimes the best way to honor God might be to toss the Bible to one side. The ancient desert fathers and mothers certainly knew this. Stories of their lives are sprinkled with accounts of them selling their most precious possession, the Bible, in order to buy food and medicines for the poor, the hungry, the orphaned, and the widowed. The Bible is to be cherished as a record of humanity's striving for God, as well as for the many spiritual insights it offers. In this sense it is indeed "God breathed." But so is the rest of creation, if we but know how to read it, because God's revelation is creatively dynamic and ongoing.

Instead of wallpapering our inner sanctums with pages from a Bible, we'd do better to make paper airplanes out of them and, riding on them, soar to new discoveries about the Lord. The wind rushing through our hair will be the Holy Spirit blowing away mental cobwebs and spiritual dust. The Bible is a necessary vehicle, but it's not the destination. It's a finger, not the moon.

Chapter 7

My god

Getting to know God is a lot like
getting to know a person. You spend
time together, whether happy or
sad. You laugh together. You weep
together. You fight and argue, then
reconcile.

—PHILIP YANCEY

Your own personal Jesus
Someone to hear your prayers
Someone who cares
Someone who's there.

—DEPECHE MODE[1]

In January 2012, a young Christian evangelist named Jefferson Bethke released a YouTube rap that immediately went viral. In its first six months "Why I Hate Religion, But Love Jesus" received twenty-two million hits.

---

[1] Philip Yancey, *Reaching for the Invisible God* (Grand Rapids, MI: Zondervan, 2000), 108; and "Personal Jesus," a 1989 single released by the musical group Depeche Mode.

Bethke's video is a two-fisted pounding of institutionalized religion. At best, he chants, religion is "just behavior modification" that "never gets to the core." At worst, it's an "infection" that enslaves and blinds. But fortunately, religion isn't the only game in town. Jesus is the saving alternative. Jesus came to "abolish religion." In contrast to religion, Jesus "sets you free" and "lets you see." How? By inviting us to enter into a personal relationship with him that's uncorrupted by the infection of religion. Staring directly into the camera, Bethke raps, "when he was dangling on that cross, he was thinking of you." Jesus wants to be *your* special friend. "This is what makes religion and Jesus two different clans."

Who of us hasn't at one time or another had it with religious rituals that come across as dry and meaningless or ecclesial authority that seems top heavy and out of touch? Because frustration with churches, denominations, and anything that smacks of formal religion is on the uptick these days, it's not surprising that Bethke's video became an overnight sensation. He speaks for hundreds of thousands when he declines what C. S. Lewis once called "whiskey and soda" or watered-down Christianity and orders his Jesus "straight up."

It's risky to insist that there's only one right way to worship God, or that any single religious tradition has a monopoly on the absolute truth. God far surpasses our ability to know or speak, and this accommodates a latitude of styles and approaches: high church, low church, no church. People like Bethke gravitate toward low and no churchiness, aiming for a personal and intimate relationship with Jesus unimpeded by what they consider to be ecclesial rigmarole. There's nothing inherently troubling, much less wrong, about this approach. It's the backbone, for example, of the Anabaptist tradition.

But things can go awry when taking Jesus straight up means that you claim him as your own personal deity. Jesus then becomes a pal with whom you're increasingly chummy, your very own therapist to whom you go for advice, a private trainer who stretches your spiritual muscles, and a personal bodyguard who watches your back. This best-friend-Jesus belongs to you *alone;* to have a *best* friend, after all, implies exclusivity. This isn't to say that Jesus doesn't have other friends besides you, but only that you're his very special friend. And the neatest thing of all is that you and he are so alike that speaking to him is really like speaking to yourself. The two of you are so intimate that you share a private language that excludes others who might want to poke their noses in. That's just how close—and closed—the relationship is.

Put in this stark way, it's hard to imagine that anyone's relationship with God could devolve in such a shocking way. But if we think about some of the phrases that are the stock-in-trade of many American evangelicals—ones like "born again," "personal relationship with Jesus," and "saved"—the unimaginable gets a little closer. That's because these terms are often coded references to a privatized deity whose primary concern is *my* life, *my* happiness, and *my* salvation. This deity is *My* god, an idol whose devotees are at the opposite end of the spectrum from worshipers of We Can Do It! god. Can Do-ers exhaust themselves in busily working for the public good. *My* godders retreat into a self-confirming and non-falsifiable subjectivity in which the only thing that matters to them is their personal relationship with the Divine. Each and every one of them is a congregation of one.

Privatizing God

Many American Christians, particularly Protestant evangelicals, complain loudly about the privatization of religion. Their gripe is that America's increasingly pluralistic culture tolerates Christians' beliefs provided that they keep them to themselves. They can worship however they wish in the privacy of their homes and churches, and they're certainly entitled to carry around in their heads whatever ideas about God they wish. But the minute they publicly witness their faith, much less wave it around as a political banner, they're accused of trying to shove it down everyone else's throat. This insistence that their beliefs be kept out of the public marketplace, they argue, not only gets in the way of their duty to spread the gospel, but it also speaks loudly about just how little they and their faith are actually respected.

I don't think there's any doubt that this complaint has some merit. Secular society's insistence that religious belief is a private matter of conscience is often a backhanded way of dismissing religion as a personal hobbyhorse or eccentricity, not something that has any real value. But ironically, a *My* godder, while often the screechiest deplorer of the privatization of religion, in fact practices an utterly privatized faith. The primary bond that links him with his god is concern for his own personal salvation. The hallmark of his god's saving approval is an intensely felt private conversion experience. Afterward, his loyalty to *My* god is so passionately single-minded that he can't but feel his god reciprocates with the same exclusivity. His entire religious life is an exaltation of this one-on-one relationship between him and his god, and he has trouble understanding or accepting any other way of relating to the Divine. His default assumption is that anyone who hasn't had a born-again experience isn't really right with God. He throws such challenges as "Have you been saved?" or "Are you born again?" or "Do you have a personal relationship with Jesus?" at others. He assumes all should take his private sense of intimacy with his god as the gold standard. He's willing to share the good news about his god with heathens and sinners, and even rejoices when they get born again. But the god who saves them first and foremost remains *his* god. He's the favorite son, the best friend, the uniquely beloved. They're the second chosen.

Worship of *My* god, like all idolatry, is motivated by fear. What drives *My* godders into the arms of their deity is panic at the thought of abandonment and aloneness. There's more need than love in their reaching out to their god. To a certain extent, they're like the person in a dysfunctional relationship who clings so intensely to the beloved out of fear of losing her that he winds up driving her away and losing the very thing he desperately wants to keep. It's difficult to tell which causes him more anxiety: losing her or being alone and unloved. At any rate, the more scared he becomes, the more he clutches; the more he clutches, the more he alienates his beloved's affections. Many of us have been on either the receiving or the giving end of this unhealthy dynamic at one time or another. It's worse than unpleasant. It's corrosive.

But the *My* godder thinks he's found a way to put the fear of abandonment to rest once and for all. He's entered into a relationship with someone who will never leave him. He's found his soul-mate—it's just that it happens to be a divine one—and there's absolutely no danger that this soul-mate will ever feel suffocated or stymied by his clinginess. In fact, the divine soul-mate actually wants the same intense and exclusive relationship that his devotee craves. *My* god *wants* to lavish an infinity of affection upon him and him alone. *My* god and his devotee staring forever into one another's eyes, shutting out the rest of the world. *Me* and *my* savior. Bliss.

A tiny handful of *My* godders may become hermits or recluses, ensuring that human company literally doesn't get between them and their god. But most of them belong to churches. Given the *My* godder's suspicion of organized religion (churches are infections, Jesus is the cure), this is surprising until one realizes two things. The first, as we've seen over and over, is that all forms of idolatry are inconsistent in one way or another, largely because the needy fear that motivates them encourages blind spots on the devotees' parts. The second is that even when *My* godders gather together as church members to worship collectively, they pretty much remain in a private world in which they and their god are the only inhabitants. When I was a teenager growing up in the South, I attended enough tent revivals to realize that by the time the preaching reached its emotional crescendo—when "the Spirit," as the preacher would say, "was let loose"—members of the congregation were present in body but not in spirit. Heads upturned, faces intense with rapture, eyes shut tight, vision turned inward, arms swaying in the air, shouts of "praise

Jesus!" flowing from their mouths: each worshiper felt swept up into the third heaven. Collective excitement under the tent may have been the catalyst, but the ecstatic experiences that followed were utterly private, each worshiper so self-absorbed that everything else melted away. The same private rapture can be observed, Sunday after Sunday, among worshipers at many of today's mega-churches. They may be standing shoulder to shoulder when they jump to their feet to shout hosannahs, but they're in no one's company but their god's.

Perhaps the most dramatic expression of this privacy in the midst of collective worship is the phenomenon of speaking in tongues (glossolalia). At the height of an ecstatic bonding between devotee and deity, the worshiper sometimes utters sounds, usually a discordant mixture of fluid and hard consonants, which are supposedly words from a sacred language. *My* god worshiper's one-on-one relationship with his deity has become so intimate that he serves as god's mouthpiece. His god speaks to others through his lips.

Or at least so he believes. But the purpose of speech is to communicate, and what flows from a glossolalic *My* godder's mouth communicates nothing. It's gibberish, lacking syntactical pattern or semantic meaning. If it *is* the language of God, God apparently ignores the universal rules of grammar that govern speech. So, whatever the devotee utters during his ecstasy is absolutely incomprehensible to the rest of us. He speaks a faux-language known only to him and his god.

My god idolatry's privatization of religious experience and its assurances that the devotee will never be abandoned are rooted in three experiences—being born again, getting saved, and developing a personal relationship with God—that are as subjective as they are inscrutable. Each of them is defiantly private, resisting any challenge by outsiders. But a *My* godder doesn't see this as a problem. For him, it only underscores the authenticity of the experience.

Take the experience of being born again, which *My* godders believe is simultaneously a bestowal of salvation. As they describe it, getting born again is always a sudden, overwhelmingly emotional experience, something like the tent-revival conversions I witnessed as a teen. The born again person feels that all her sins have been instantaneously expunged (she's been "washed in the blood of the Lamb"), and her past wiped clean. Pure as the day she was born, she's a new person, spiritually reborn and saved in a single swoop. It's not surprising that this instantaneous bestowal of such an incredible gift—one, moreover, she believes is totally undeserved—leads her to the conviction that she and the god who gives it are in a special relationship. As one of my born-again students once told me, she and Jesus "are going steady."

Now, there are undoubtedly real experiences of instant conversion. Saint Paul's sudden turnabout testifies to such possibilities. But today we know enough about the psychology of conversion to understand that most conversions are cumulative rather than out of the blue, and that intensely emotional born-again conversions often burn themselves out over time. Whether or not they endure, they remain inescapably subjective. Being born again and feeling saved are matters of private conviction and interpretation. We all know how easily we can be mistaken when it comes to matters of fact about which we're relatively indifferent. The danger of misinterpreting a personal experience in which we're heavily invested is even greater. The intensity of a belief in no way guarantees its truth. In fact, it ought to put us on alert for the possibility of wishful thinking. Most of us have learned this lesson from sad experience.

Or consider the *My* godder foundational experience of achieving a "personal relationship" with God. Obviously, it suffers from the same subjectivism that born again and saved experiences do, since no one but the devotee knows what kind of a relationship with the Divine she has. But the problem of subjectivism to one side, there are two additional perplexities here.

The first is that it's not at all clear what it means to have a "personal relationship" with God. We have firsthand knowledge, of course, about what it means to have a personal relationship with another person: we're emotionally and/ or sexually intimate, we trust each other, we share common interests and have fun when we're together, we squabble occasionally and then reconcile, we go to movies or lie in bed reading the Sunday newspapers, protect each other from danger but sometimes join forces to bully or intimidate others, we travel together, share secrets, and so on. Our partner is a concrete, tangible human being, and so is our relationship.

Now, when *My* godders talk about a personal relationship with their god, they obviously mean that they have a special bond of trustful intimacy with him analogous but spiritually superior to the kind found in human personal relationships. But other than that generality, what could they mean? Evangelical author Philip Yancey says that in such a personal relationship "you spend time together, whether happy or sad. You laugh together. You weep together. You fight and argue, then reconcile." But surely this stretches the analogy to the breaking point. God laughs and weeps? God bickers? God gets sad? Language like this is singularly unhelpful in trying to make sense of the "personal relationship" experience.

The second problem is an offshoot of the first. Once the *My* godder begins ascribing to God person-like qualities like Yancy's, he risks "ungodding" God, draining God of the transcendence and mystery that mark him as God rather than human in the first place. In striving to make sense of "personal," he reduces God to a person. But an experience of God, as the German theologian Rudolf Otto insightfully noted, ought to overwhelm us with awe and fascination, and both of them come from being bowled over by God's majesty and sheer other-ness.[2] We can trust as a matter of faith that God loves us and wishes the best for us, we can occasionally feel the Divine's love, and we can reciprocate as best we can. But God will never be our pal, much less our peer, for the simple reason that God is God.

---

[2] Rudolf Otto, *The Idea of the Holy* (London: Oxford University Press, 1923).

A wonderfully funny scene from the 1999 film *Dogma* drives home just how absurd it is to "ungod" God by turning him into a best friend. (If you haven't seen the movie, by the way, put down this book and watch it! It's brilliant, but be prepared for some salty language.) Comedian George Carlin plays Cardinal Glick, a prelate of the Roman Catholic Church who calls a press conference to announce a new evangelization campaign. Traditional images of God, he tells the gathered jounalists, no longer speak to people. They're too distant or too gloomy. Who wants to look at creepy crucifixes these days? What people want is a god they can feel close to, talk to, relate to in an up close and personal way. So to fill that need, Glick announces a new image—Buddy Jesus—and proudly unveils a statue designed to replace conventional Christian symbols: a life-size plaster figure of Jesus pointing to the crowd with one hand, giving a thumbs-up with the other, grinning hugely, and waggishly winking. Now *there's* a god we can relate to, a god we wouldn't mind downing a beer with at the corner tavern. Buddy Jesus.

The only problem, of course, is that Buddy Jesus isn't God. He's a graven image of *My* god, which in turn is actually a graven image of *My* godder. As we saw in Chapter One, what an idolater really worships is an idealized projection of himself or herself. In no other form of idolatry is this more obvious than devotion to *My* god. After all, what kind of relationship can be more personal or up close—not to mention private—than a relationship with ourselves? Theologian David Wells puts his finger on the obsessive narcissism of *My* god idolaters. They labor, he writes,

> under the illusion that the God they make in the image of the self becomes more real as he more nearly comes to resemble the self, to accommodate its needs and desires. The truth is quite the opposite. It is ridiculous to assert that God could become more real by abandoning his own character in an effort to identify more completely

with ours. And yet the illusion has proved compelling to an entire generation.[3]

Our God

An Episcopal priest friend of mine tells me that whenever she hears members of her congregation refer to "my" Jesus, she gently reminds them that he's *our* Jesus. Her observation that no one has a monopoly on God sometimes startles her parishioners. On an abstract level, of course, they know perfectly well that *their* God is also *everybody's* God. But on a visceral level the temptation to think of God as exclusively their own is never too distant. This doesn't necessarily make them *My* godders, but it does suggest that they have tendencies in that direction. The truth of the matter is that most of us probably do. This is partly because of the rugged individualism that's so much a part of the American ethos—our programmed tendency to think in terms of *me* rather than *us*—but more fundamentally because fear of being alone is pretty primal. What separates *My* godders from the rest of us isn't their dread of aloneness, but the way in which they deal with it.

I said earlier that *My* godders are so frightened of abandonment that they *need*, more than *love*, their god. That's true, but it needs to be qualified. As C. S. Lewis noted, there's always (or at least ought to be) an element of need whenever humans turn to God. Agreeing with Plato that need is "the son of poverty," Lewis concluded that it is "the accurate reflection in consciousness of our actual nature. We are born helpless. As soon as we are fully conscious we discover loneliness."[4] Moreover, he argued, it won't do to pretend that need and love are two completely separate things, even

---

[3] David Wells, *God in the Wasteland* (Grand Rapids, MI: Eerdmans, 1994), 100–101.

[4] C. S. Lewis, *The Four Loves* (Boston: Houghton Mifflin Harcourt, 1991), 2.

though we often speak in ordinary conversation as if they are. Since all of us dread aloneness, our loves—and even our causal acquaintanceships, for that matter—must be motivated at least partly by need. And if that's the case, how could our love for God not also reflect our need for companionship?

This seems reasonable. But the need of a *My* godder is excessive because his or her fear is excessive. Sometimes, as Lewis says, need can be monstrous, a "tyrannous and gluttonous demand for affection."[5] Remember the demanding lover whose need suffocates the beloved? Lewis's choice of the word *gluttonous* is particularly illuminating here. *My* godders' fear of aloneness makes them so greedy for God, the ultimate guarantee against abandonment, that they hog God all to themselves. Surely this is need that's spiraled out of control into gluttony. A reasonable person can need something without demanding all of it. My thirst shouldn't lead me to demand all the potable water the world has to offer. This is not only foolish, since I can never drink it all myself, but it's also improper, because I have no exclusive right to the world's water. Everyone gets thirsty. It's not *my* water, any more than it's *my* Jesus. It's *our* water, and *our* Jesus.

But gluttonous *My* godders tend to elbow other people away from the divine feeding trough. They don't want to share their god with others because they vaguely fear that doing so will spread their god too thin and thereby diminish their personal relationship with him. But what they fail to note is that even though God is the *primary* human need, God isn't the *sole* human need. The loneliness into which we're born craves God, but also the companionship of fellow humans, of flesh-and-blood creatures whom we see face to face, whose bodies we touch, whose voices we hear. In pushing them to the periphery lest they somehow get between him and his god, the *My* godder actually fuels rather than tamps down his sense of aloneness. The consequence can be a life in which Buddy Jesus becomes a burden rather than a blessing.

---

[5] Ibid., 3.

Data recently collected from evangelical clergy who claim a born-again personal relationship with Jesus bleakly attest to this possibility: 50 percent of them divorce; 70 percent battle depression; fifteen hundred leave the ministry each month because of burnout; and 50 percent of those who stay in want out.[6]

So worship of *My* god, like all forms of idolatry, winds up pushing devotees exactly where they don't wish to go— ever deeper into the loneliness they need to escape. What their idolatry won't allow them to recognize is that God is everyone's (or, better, that everyone is God's), not just theirs, and that accordingly all humans are joined together in fellowship not just with God but with one another, too. In the Christian tradition all believers are in Christ. Christ lives in and through them, and this not only binds each one of them to God but also to one another. Our proper relationship to God is cruciform, horizontal as well as vertical. It includes a private dimension but also a social one. Each of us is a child of God, but together we are the children of God and siblings to one another. When we look into one another's face, we should discern traces of our common Parent's lineaments. Others don't get in the way of a "personal relationship" with God. They enhance it.

In a well-known passage from *Conjectures of a Guilty Bystander* Thomas Merton, who himself struggled with *My* god tendencies, describes the moment when he realized this truth. It happened one day as he stood on the corner of Fourth and Walnut Street in Louisville, Kentucky. He'd gone to town from the quiet and solitude of Gethsemani monastery for some dental work, and the bustling crowds of people on the sidewalk initially dazed him. But then, he tells us, "I was suddenly overwhelmed with the realization that I loved all those people, that they were mine and I theirs, that we could not be alien to one another even though we were total strangers. It was like waking from a dream of separateness,

---

[6] Richard J. Krejcir, "Statistics on Pastors," Shaeffer Institute (2007).

of spurious self-isolation." The epiphany revealed to him that even though he, as a monk, had a special relationship with God, so did everyone else. Monks may be more conscious of the relationship, "but does that entitle us to consider ourselves different, or even better, than others? The whole idea is preposterous."[7]

"Liberated" from the "illusory" assumption that his relationship with God was somehow exclusively his own, realizing that the God he worshiped belonged to everyone equally, Merton was able to appreciate more fully the significance of the incarnation. Because "God Himself gloried in becoming a member of the human race," God was still present in every human being that Merton encountered. "I saw the secret beauty of their hearts, the depths of their hearts where neither sin nor desire nor self-knowledge can reach, the core of their reality, the person that each one is in God's eyes." This freed Merton to embrace the truth that God is always *our* God, discernible in every person we meet, and the exclusive possession of no one.[8]

Merton's insight harkens back to one of the oldest of Christian traditions, the notion that all of us are members of the body of Christ. Paul introduced the image in his first letter to the Corinthians: "For just as the body is one and has many members, and all the members of the body, though many, are one body, so it is with Christ. For in one Spirit we were all baptized into one body . . . Indeed, the body does not consist of one member but of many" (12:12–14). Paul goes on to say that the members of Christ's body, like the limbs and organs of a person's physical body, cooperate with one another and profit from one another's unique gifts. So in order to avoid discord, members must care for one another. "If one member suffers, all suffer together with it; if one member is honored, all rejoice together with it" (12:26).

---

[7] Thomas Merton, *Conjectures of a Guilty Bystander* (New York: Image, 1968), 154.

[8] Ibid., 154, 155.

If Paul is correct, there simply is no such thing as an exclusive relationship with God. My relationship with God affects the entire body of believers—one might even say, the entire cosmos—just as their relationships affect me. My personal relationship with God inevitably incorporates all of God's children. My proper concern can't be my salvation alone, but the salvation of the entire groaning and travailing universe. Once I embrace my membership in the body of Christ, I would no more dream of demanding an exclusive relationship with God than I would of claiming as my own all of the world's potable water. I recognize, as Merton did, that the long loneliness that makes me needy for God also, and quite properly, invites me to embrace my fellow humans, all members of *our* God's body.

Chapter 8

Church god

You cannot keep Christ in your Churches; He will break them into pieces if you try. He will make for the streets in spite of you.
—G. A. STUDDERT KENNEDY[1]

Here's the church,
Here's the steeple,
Open the doors,
And see all the people!
—A CHILDREN'S RHYME

I'll remember it as long as I live: the occasion, several years ago now, when an elderly parishioner, still hale and hearty but looking toward the future, sat down to discuss her funeral plans with me. She told me the hymns she wanted sung and the scripture passages she wanted read. All of it was pretty

---

[1] G. A. Studdert Kennedy, *The Wicket Gate* (London: Hodder and Stoughton, 1923). Although sadly neglected today, Studdert Kennedy was one of the early twentieth-century's most exciting theologians. An anthology of his work may be found in *After War, Is Faith Possible? The Life and Message of Geoffrey "Woodbine Willie" Studdert Kennedy,* ed. Kerry Walters (Eugene, OR: Wipf and Stock, 2008).

standard stuff. But then she said something unusual: "I want my *Book of Common Prayer* (the Episcopal missal) buried with me."

My immediate thought was that her prayer book, well thumbed from decades of continuous use, had so much sentimental value that she couldn't bear to part with it even in death. But then she went on to explain that she'd need it where she was headed, because heaven was going to be one unending church service. My first impulse was to blurt out: "You think you'll be going to *church* in heaven?!" My second was to ask, "An *Episcopal* church?" But I kept my mouth shut and dutifully made a note of her request. (As of this writing, by the way, she's still very much alive and approaching her ninetieth year.)

Even though I think her vision of heaven is pretty unlikely, I get why she finds it so attractive. There's something reassuringly cozy about the thought of spending eternity in a place that's pretty much like your parish church. You'll feel right at home, forever sitting in your accustomed spot in the pew, forever reciting the familiar liturgical responses, forever walking up to the altar rail to receive the sacrament, forever singing the hymns known by heart, and for all I know, forever enjoying coffee hour afterward. Maybe there'll even be a celestial altar guild to join (but, since this is heaven, no vestry or finance committee.) It's all very quaint and comfortable and innocent enough.

What's a bit disturbing, though, is the fact that my parishioner holds her particular denominational home in such high regard that she just naturally presumes that God and all the heavenly hosts are fellow Episcopalians. It bespeaks an inflated reverence for the worldly institution we generically call *The Church*. By the term I mean the entire ecclesial ethos—architecture, customs, traditions, liturgies, and hierarchies, regardless of denomination—that, unchecked, conflates church and God. Such a conflation morphs the living God (who, truth to tell, isn't much of a churchman at all) into Church god. It's an easy idolatry to slip into; clergy as well

as laity succumb to it. "Churcholatry" is a special temptation for members of established mainstream and hierarchical
denominations who become so wrapped up in The Church's
daily life and business that they begin to identify them with
God's will and God's presence. It's a short-sightedness born
from such a total immersion in and identification with The
Church that the infinite distance between God and human
institutions somehow gets forgotten.

Spiritual agoraphobia

There are several varieties of churcholaters, ranging from relatively harmless church mice to very dangerous Torquemadas.
But before we explore them, it's helpful to think about the
fear that drives all of them into the arms of their god.

An observation made by nineteenth-century philosopher
John Stuart Mill can start us on our way. He said that people
generally fall into two camps. Some folks crave lives of excitement, adventure, and novelty. They're especially susceptible
to boredom and restlessness, and so are more than willing to
go out on sometimes very wobbly limbs to keep the adrenalin
flowing. Their deepest longing is for a life of intensely lived
experiences, even if that means taking risks that can shorten
their number of years. They're buccaneers.

Other people—perhaps the majority of us, although Mill
doesn't actually say this—crave a more settled existence.
Climbing up sheer rock faces or risking huge loses on a throw
of the dice at either Las Vegas or Wall Street isn't for them.
What they prefer is the familiar, the everyday, the comfort of
routine. It's not that they're boring or unimaginative people.
They just have personalities that predispose them to stay in
one place, figuratively and perhaps literally as well, and become part of its landscape. They're homebodies.[2]

Mill makes it quite clear that neither of these two groups is
better than the other. Which of the two any of us belongs to

---

[2] For the distinction, see John Stuart Mill, *Utilitarianism* (1863).

is largely a matter of temperament. Our inclination to one or the other might also be correlated with age; many of us tend to be more averse to risk in our older than in our younger years. But again, being a buccaneer or a homebody is morally neutral in and of itself. It's just the way we're built.

Problems arise, however, if either of these two temperamental predispositions become so exaggerated that they begin to damage our well-being or the well-being of those around us. A buccaneer can become so fixated on avoiding the humdrum of everyday life that she develops claustrophobia. She feels so stifled, so trapped, by everyday routine that she takes unnecessary and irresponsible risks just for the thrill. Moreover, the danger inevitably escalates because each exploit demands an even more stimulating follow-up. What seemed exciting yesterday becomes stale tomorrow. Been there, done that.

On the other hand, a homebody, who is temperamentally inclined toward the familiar and predictable, can slide into agoraphobia. The stereotype of an agoraphobic is that she fears open spaces. But more accurately, an agoraphobic is someone who falls apart in strange surroundings. The prospect of travel, of even temporarily leaving the home and hearth she knows so well, can paralyze her with dread. Any novelty that comes along to break her routine may provoke a major discombobulation. Meeting new people is cause for panic. Simply being in a crowd of anonymous strangers—at the theater, in a subway, in the dentist's waiting room—can trigger an anxiety attack. Just like claustrophobia, agoraphobia tends to get worse over time. The more the agoraphobic clings to the familiar, the less able she is to cope with novelty.

A devotee of Church god is a homebody whose need for the familiar has mushroomed into what might be called spiritual agoraphobia. Already temperamentally inclined toward a safely predictable existence, her denominational affiliation becomes such a reassuringly stable center of gravity in her life that she nests deeply within it and gradually loses the inclination and ability to think beyond its borders. External challenges to The

Church anger and distress her, internal dissent bewilders and agitates her, and change of any kind threatens her. Ecclesial contention—debates over sexual morality, for example—push the churcholater into despairing nostalgia for the good old days when The Church was of a single mind. But even relatively minor breaks in routine, such as slight liturgical innovations, can send her into a tailspin.

Her spiritual agoraphobia is so profound that she needs The Church to remain the way "it's always been." Within it, her life is ordered, regular, and predictable. The Church tells her how, when, and where to worship, and what's proper and improper, righteous and wicked. The Church bestows an identity upon her and offers her an unthreatening fellowship of familiar faces (even though occasionally the presence of newcomers temporarily disconcerts her). It anchors her present to the past by rooting her in unchanging and hoary tradition, and to the future by assuring her that heaven is very much like what she's grown accustomed to in The Church. From cradle to grave, The Church orients her, instructs her, comforts her, and protects her. She clings to it with a fierce loyalty born of fear and need, never dreaming of questioning it—and scandalized when others do. She is a Churchwoman through and through. For her, The Church is The Final Authority. The battle cry of By-the-Book-god devotees, it will be remembered, is "The Bible says it, I believe it, that settles it!" Worshipers of Church god counter with: "The Church says it, I believe it, that settles it!" By the Bookers deify a book. Churcholaters deify The Church.

From church mice to church lions

What are the different types of churcholaters?

Some are church mice. Every parish has one or more laypersons who seem to spend most of their waking life in the pew, confessional booth, sacristy, or rectory. They just can't get enough of church or clergy, whom they frequently engage in long heart-to-hearts about any and everything. They're

such a fixture in the church that their rare absence is notice-
able, sometimes evoking mild alarm but more often a certain
measure of relief. When they're not praying in a pew—and
they often admit to being unable to pray anywhere except in
church—or cornering the pastor, they eagerly offer themselves
as sacristans, Sunday School teachers, vestry members, and
general factotums. They lovingly polish brass altar rails and
painstakingly stitch prayer cushions, and they can sit for
hours staring adoringly at stained-glass windows and oaken
ceilings. Their favorite aromas are candle wax and incense.

Of course, not every layperson who haunts church buildings is necessarily a churcholater. Luke, for example, admir-
ingly mentions Anna, a widow who "never left the temple
but worshiped there with fasting and prayer night and day"
(2:37). What separates the church mouse from an Anna is
spiritual agoraphobia. The church mouse becomes a fixture
inside a church because of his need to feel safe from the unpredictable and the unfamiliar. Outside of the church building,
he feels anxious because God seems distant. Inside it, he's
protected on all sides by the presence of the Divine. But an
Anna, although she prefers praying and fasting in a church,
sees the structure as a means, not an end. If there's anything
special about the building, it's that it's been dedicated to God
and worshiped in by generations of believers. But it's entirely
expendable, even though its loss would be sad, because God
isn't confined to a particular building. God is found everywhere, and sometimes more readily outside than inside a
church structure.

The church mouse's shrinkage of God into a particular
building may impoverish his spiritual life but generally harms
no one else. But another kind of churcholater, the "company
man," does. Church mice are always laypersons, but company
men, who can be female as well as male, are often ordained.

Company men churcholaters work in one way or another
for The Church, although they're not necessarily salaried.
They can be deacons, priests and pastors, bishops, cardinals,
and even popes. They can also be Sunday School teachers, lay

preachers, retreat leaders, administrators, wardens, treasurers, secretaries, sextons, and vestry members. What they have in common is that their first and foremost source of identity is their association with The Church, just as their primary loyalty, one that trumps all others, is to The Church.

Church mice find a safe haven in actual church buildings and the reassuringly regular activities that go on within them. Company men find their security in the teachings, doctrines, administrative structures, and hierarchies of their denomination. They've never met a decree handed down by The Church that they disagreed with, and they've never failed to distrust and repudiate any idea that disagrees with what The Church says. To their minds, their denomination's catechism offers an exhaustive source of everything that ought to be believed. Similarly, the latest pastoral letters from church leaders or councils are fail-safe guides for what to think and say when it comes to moral, political, social, and doctrinal matters.

Company men think whatever The Church instructs them to think, pure and simple. In a frightening sort of way, they are not unlike members of the alien race called the Borg in the *Star Trek* television series. Remember them? Physically, they're individuals, but they share a common mind by virtue of being connected to a single central brain. They are drones within a hive, thinking (if it can be called that) and behaving only as the central brain instructs them. Put a company man in a futuristic space costume and you'd swear he was a Borg.

Is any Christian who embraces the official pronouncements of her church a company man? Not so long as she's made an effort to reflect on them rather than adopting a lockstep "The Church says it, I believe it" attitude. No denomination in its better moments wants to encourage this kind of hive thinking, and no individual believer, unless driven to it by spiritual agoraphobia, should want to relinquish the right to examine critically the doctrines and teachings of her church. Not everything her denomination teaches may carry equal weight. Some may be irrelevant holdovers from a past that's long gone, and some may strike individual believers as downright misguided.

But none of these blips show up on the company man's radar. If he once allows himself to question The Church, the panic-inducing specter of the unfamiliar leers and gibbers at him. Church doctrine and teaching are the planks from which his cozily familiar home is constructed. To call any of them into question is to risk ripping out a wall or two. It never occurs to him to worry about dry rot.

All company men hotly defend The Church against both internal and external detractors. Many a family holiday meal that started out as a happy occasion has hit a brick wall because a company man at the table got riled up by some-one's criticism of The Church. Company men are especially troubled when youngsters express innocent doubts about the denominations in which they've been raised and curiosity about alternative ones. Such questioning is both likely and healthy in teenagers, but it rattles any agoraphobic chucho-later for whom absolute fidelity to The Church is crucial.

Another characteristic of company men is that they're endlessly fascinated by everything that goes on within The Church and relatively indifferent to much of what goes on in the outside world—unless, of course, it directly affects The Church. Like corporate company men, they both live for the job and know the minutest details about their organization's canons, chains of authority, prerequisites, and customs. They delight in endlessly rehashing ecclesial gossip and speculation. If they belong to a liturgical denomination, they tend to be persnickety and pedantic in a preciously churchy sort of way. They can debate for hours whether oil candles are superior to wax ones, if the Gospel ought to be read or sung, or just how high off the floor the bottom hem of an alb should be. The intensity of these churchy discussions often strikes an outsider as so much squandered energy, especially when weighed against outside-the-church problems like gang wars and poverty. But to a churcholator, they're theology in the most literal sense of the word. If The Church is his god, then talking about the inner workings of The Church, no matter how tedious, trivial, or arcane the topic, is actually discoursing about the Divine.

Most company men, as their name suggests, remain rank and file. But a few become "lions of The Church." Some of them are scholars who write bestselling books. Others specialize in evangelization, holding nationwide revival crusades or preaching regularly on radio and television. Still others become elders and bishops, members of The Church's management team charged with safeguarding doctrine, watchdogging the faithful, and sometimes keeping the lid on internal scandals. Regardless of what specific function they perform, these leaders are in the business of making sure that The Church remains The Final Authority. It's their job to see to it that the institution is enduringly stable. They're like those sculpted guardian lions that serve as gatekeepers at Chinese temples and palaces.

Dostoyevsky gives us a searing portrait of one of these lions of The Church in his parable "The Grand Inquisitor." The tale is set in Seville at the time of the Inquisition. Jesus has returned to earth. As he walks up and down the streets in silence, the common folk, especially children, recognize him immediately and cluster around him. Once Torquemada, the Grand Inquisitor, gets word of this, he orders his soldiers to seek out Jesus, snatch him away from the crowds, and bring him to the cathedral.

You'd think a religious leader would be overjoyed at Jesus's return. But Torquemada is a lion of The Church, and his response is ferocious. He's furious that Jesus has come back, fearing that his presence undermines the authority and power of the institution to which Torquemada belongs and to which he has pledged his ultimate loyalty. As Jesus stands before him, silent and in chains, the Grand Inquisitor launches into a venomous tirade against the gift of freedom that Jesus tried to give humanity. Humans don't want freedom, a disdainful Torquemada insists. On the contrary, they crave the very three temptations that Jesus resisted in the wilderness.

They want their bellies filled, they want authority figures to tell them what to do, and they want to be razzle-dazzled with supernatural tricks. Freedom is too onerous because it always brings with it ambiguity, risk, and responsibility.

Thankfully, Torquemada says, The Church in its wisdom has managed to lessen the burden of freedom that Jesus misguidedly offered humanity. Its decrees and doctrines, its comforting tales of miracles and saints, and above all its authority, are exactly what people want. It's taken centuries to overcome the ill effects of Jesus's influence, and the Grand Inquisitor isn't about to let all The Church's labor be undone. So tomorrow, he promises, Jesus will be taken to the city square. Once there, the very people who rejoiced at his second coming will hasten, at The Church's command, "to heap up the hot cinders about the pile on which I shall burn Thee for coming to hinder us. For if anyone has ever deserved our fires, it is Thou. To-morrow I shall burn Thee. *Dixi* [I have spoken!]."[3]

The imperious *Dixi* is a nice touch on Dostoyevsky's part. It's like a steel door slamming shut. Once The Church speaks, there's an end to the matter once and for all. Further discussion, much less dissent, is intolerable. And to make sure that the door stays shut, lions of The Church like Torquemada crouch outside it—when, that is, they're not on the prowl looking for troublemaking prey.

None of us wants to believe that any religious leader would respond to Jesus the way Torquemada does. But Doestoyevsky's parable is a reminder of how lions tend to ignore Jesus's teachings in order to make The Church a power to be reckoned with. Jesus preached absolute non-violence. Lions solemnly bless armed conflict. Jesus taught the virtue of voluntary poverty. Lions want The Church to be immensely wealthy. Jesus taught humility and meekness. Lions downplay them. Jesus taught servant-leadership. Lions

---

of The Church overlook the servant part. Above all, Jesus taught the two great commandments. But lions add a third: love of The Church. For them, as a matter of fact, God and neighbor take second place to the stability and continuation of The Church. The Church must be protected, a lion says, come what may. *Dixi.*

It mustn't be supposed that Lions of The Church are sinister and corrupt figures out for their own gain. They may be misguided, and their fierce loyalty to The Church god may cause a good deal of damage. But they're not charlatans or hypocrites. Dostoyevsky's Torquemada isn't a Pope Julius II or an Elmer Gantry. He genuinely believes that The Church he serves brings peace of mind and material prosperity to the masses, and he desperately wants to guard against anything that threatens what he sees as the world's last line of defense against the savagery of misused freedom. He is a tireless man of conscience who devotes himself wholeheartedly to his god. But as we've seen over and over, if the god one follows is an idol, the service inevitably corrupts the devotee and might well inflict damage upon others.

Another literary allegory, this one William Golding's *The Spire,* likewise portrays the dangerous arrogance of churcholatry. The dark novel is set in the Middle Ages in the English town of Salisbury. Jocelin, dean of Salisbury Cathedral, is obsessed with adding another four hundred feet to the cathedral's already perilously tall spire. "I've waited half my life for this day!" he joyfully exclaims when construction, long delayed by lack of funds and workmen, finally begins. But not everyone shares his excitement. The master builder in charge of the project warns him again and again that the cathedral's foundation can't support the additional weight. He reveals that he's already heard the ribbed columns supporting the sanctuary roof ominously "singing" under the strain. No matter how artful his masons and carpenters are, "sooner or later there'd be a bang, a shudder, a roar. Those four columns would open apart like a flower, and everything else up here, stone, wood, iron, glass, men, would slide down into the church like the fall of a mountain."[4]

But Jocelin refuses to heed the warnings. To his mind, the spire is Church god's finger pointing heavenward. Increasing the height of the spire adds to the majesty of the cathedral and the awe-inspiring authority of The Church, and both embody and glorify Jocelin's god. No matter that the project is dangerous, consumes chests of gold that otherwise could feed and clothe the poor and sick, and is almost certainly doomed to failure. Come what may, Jocelin will serve his god by dressing him in new finery. He will build a spire that can be seen from miles away, a spire that, like The Church, towers high above ordinary men and women to awe them with its grandeur.

But, of course, Jocelin's spire, like the biblical tower of Babel, comes to a bad end. The twists and turns of its construction destroy several lives, including Jocelin's, and the inevitability of the spire's collapse is darkly insinuated more than once in the novel. By the end of the tale, Jocelin's dedication to Church god has harmed the very institution he hoped to serve. Close to death, he realizes that he has lost every scrap of faith he once had in Church god. Everything in the world strikes him as empty, ordinary, and sad. All that he has left is a mortar and stone building creaking and groaning under its own top-heavy weight, ready at any minute to come crashing to the ground.

Called-out people

Many of us remember the nursery rhyme that begins "Here's the church, here's the steeple." We chanted it as kids, making a church with our interlocked fingers before turning our hands upside down and wiggling our fingers to show "all the people." It was just a silly bit of fun when I was a youngster.

---

[4] William Golding, *The Spire* (New York: Harcourt, Brace, and World, 1964), 3, 113.

But now that I'm older (and, I hope, a little wiser), the rhyme strikes me as a wonderful image of what the church, as opposed to The Church, really is. It's not spires and steeples, whether made of stone and steel, words and documents, or regulations and hierarchies. It's the people, the wiggling fingers, who come together to worship God. They're the church.

Our forebears appreciated this long before there were church buildings or ecclesial institutions. The word *church* is derived from a Greek verb meaning "to call people together." The folks who assemble in response to the call are literally the called-out people. From the very beginning church was thought of as a community of people bound by a shared calling. That calling, of course, was faith that the historical man Jesus somehow embodied the eternal God, and that his life, death, and resurrection offered humanity the chance of a fresh start. Moreover, the called-out people distinguished themselves from the rest of the world by living according to the values Jesus preached: profligate love for God and everyone else, even enemies; voluntary simplicity; compassion for the underdog; hope. The love that united the called-out people and fueled their practice of Jesus's teachings made them a bit freer from the worst snares of ego, anger, and greed than they otherwise would have been.

But no one ever claimed that the assembly of called-out people was The Final Authority. People are people, even when God calls them out. The best remain fallible, despite their good intentions. If they become leaders, their power only increases the possibility of error, or worse. And as for the rest of us, we muddle along as best we can. Like Saint Paul, we often do the worse even when wanting with all our hearts to do the better. Being a called-out people doesn't make us or the institutions we create perfect. We rise and we fall, rise and fall. But because we're people called out by a risen Lord, we hope to rise again after each fall. We may stand upon rock, and we may have faith that the rock will ultimately support us. But we also know that our legs are wobbly.

Perhaps the deep-down, queasy-making awareness of this inescapable wobbliness feeds the spiritual agoraphobia of churcholaters. Is it the wide-open spaces within themselves, those savannahs of uncertainty and ambivalence—in other words, the God-given gift of freedom rejected by Torquemada—that they truly fear? Or is it the wide-open space of the living God who refuses to be crammed into neat categories and classifications, much less into sealed containers like church buildings? Both, most likely. But whatever its darkest, most hidden roots may be, spiritual agoraphobia transforms the church into The Church, mutating it from a called-out people who freely worship the living God as best they can into a god worshiped and thought about in ways predictably routine, safely prescribed, and frozenly institutionalized

Yet Dostoyevsky reminds us that a deep nostalgia for freedom endures, even in the most clamped-down churcholator. At the end of his parable about Jesus and the Grand Inquisitor, after Jesus is told he'll be executed in the morning, something unexpected happens. Jesus, who has been wordless throughout the entire tale, walks over to Torquemada and silently kisses him. The old man shudders, throws open the prison door, and bids Jesus to leave and never return. But afterward, says Dostoyevsky, "the kiss glowed in his heart." Is it too much to believe that the kiss is that seismic event which eventually will shatter Torquemada's churcholatry? And if there's hope for such a ferocious lion of The Church, there's hope for church mice and company men too.

Chapter 9

Designer god

We worship not the Graces, nor the Parcae, but Fashion. She spins and weaves and cuts with full authority.

—Henry David Thoreau

When I use a word, it means just what I choose it to mean—neither more nor less.

—Humpty Dumpty[1]

The Philosophers' Magazine, a quarterly journal published in England, sponsors an online game called Do-It-Yourself Deity. Players are invited to pick the characteristics they think any respectable god should possess. After they're chosen, a "crack team of metaphysical engineers" analyzes the selections, creates a profile of the god they add up to, and then assesses the likelihood of that god's existence. The team bases this final determination on whether the do-it-yourself

---

[1] Henry David Thoreau, *Walden,* in *The Portable Thoreau,* ed. Jeffrey S. Cramer (New York: Penguin, 2012), 217 (the Parcae are also known as the Fates, female personifications of destiny); Lewis Carroll, *Through the Looking Glass, and What Alice Found There* (1871), chap. 6.

deity is compatible with what we know about the nature of the universe, and whether the divine qualities chosen by the player are consistent with one another.

The game is fun—I recommend playing it—but like most things in *The Philosophers' Magazine,* it has a serious bent too. The designers of the game are interested in figuring out if the qualities we traditionally attribute to God stand up under rational scrutiny. Is omnipotence a self-contradicting quality—for example, would it mean that God is powerful enough to create something over which God has no control? Can divine goodness be squared with innocent suffering in the world? These are the sorts of questions that philosophers and theologians have pondered for centuries. They're the same ones most of us wrestle with at one time or another in our lives.

The take-away lesson from the Do-It-Yourself Deity game is this: ideas about God have to be reality-checked. Divine attributes mustn't contradict one another; they have to make sense. That's the point the game explicitly makes. You can't, for example, claim that God is good while at the same time saying that God is responsible for evil, unless you do some serious finessing with the terms *good* and *evil.* The game's second point is less explicit but just as crucial: you can't claim that God is just whatever you want God to be or think God ought to be. Doing so puts God at the mercy of whimsy, transforming God from an objectively real entity into a subjective invention fashioned by passing moods or the latest spiritual fad. Today, since I'm in a pretty good mood, I want God to be peace loving. Tomorrow, when I get annoyed at someone, I'll want God to be vengeful. Today, I want God to be the New Testament Jesus. Tomorrow, after reading a book on Hinduism, I want God to be a combo of Jesus and Krishna. The day after that, I may toss a bit of Shinto or Buddhism into the hopper. Who knows?

What exactly is the problem here? After all, God is essentially mysterious, and we only just glimpse God when the darkness is briefly lit by flashes of divine revelation and human insight. It follows that all our attempts to speak about God necessarily fall woefully short of description, and that the best we can hope to do is find words that gesture at a reality that forever runs ahead of them. As Flannery O'Connor once wrote, Jesus is the ragged figure who flits from tree to tree in the back of our minds.[2]

Fair enough. But acknowledging God's elusiveness is a far cry from assuming that God changes, chameleon-like, to suit our every passing fancy. In our less reflective moods that may be what we want God to do. But it doesn't take long for most of us to conclude that this kind of God is no God at all. It's just a self-indulgent piece of wishful thinking

Most, but not all. Some of us never move beyond a desire to piece together a god especially designed to match our mercurial whims or latest interests. So we patchwork our deity together, stitching up a scrap from here and a piece from there, heedless of how ill-suited for one another they may be. We make sure to sew the seams loosely, because we reserve the right to rip out old arrangements and begin anew as the mood hits us or as god-fashions change. We don't want to commit ourselves to a single divine model or to be caught wearing last year's theological or spiritual clothes after the new season arrives. The first cramps our style, and the second is embarrassing. How totally yesterday.

People who think about God along these lines are devotees of Designer god, an idol whose essence might be best represented by a naked mannequin ready to be draped in whatever clothes a devotee chooses to dress him, and just as ready to be reclothed whenever the devotee changes her mind. All of us have run across people who, when asked what they think heaven is likely to be, somewhat dreamily respond: "Heaven is just whatever each person wants it to be." A "Designerist"

---

[2] Flannery O'Connor, *Wise Blood* (New York: Farrar, Straus, and Giroux, 2007), 16.

goes one better. Following the lead of that rotund man of letters Humpty Dumpty, the word *god* means nothing more or less than what she wants it to mean.

God walls

Someone who might've gotten a kick out of the Do-It-Yourself Deity game is the twentieth-century philosopher Jean-Paul Sartre, one of the most influential atheists of his generation. Sartre's denial of God's existence was based on his intuition that if the universe is created by a divine intelligence, there must be a cosmic blueprint that predefines the nature of everything, including humans. In other words, everything that comes into being already has a specific and unchangeable essence determined by God and neatly catalogued in the book of nature. We humans may not know what that nature is in every case—for example, we've squabbled for centuries over how to define our own nature—but if God exists, we have one.

This kind of pre-set definition may be fine for inanimate objects and nonhuman animals. But what Sartre objected to was the ordaining of *human* nature. If we're born with a specific nature that *must* be ours by virtue of our humanity, he argued, then we aren't free to create our own identities through our actions and decisions in the world. We're hemmed in by God walls, forever imprisoned in the metaphysical pigeonhole into which God shoved our blueprints when he planned the universe. Sartre considered this a deal breaker when it comes to believing in God, first because it violates our everyday sense of free will and second because creating predetermined humans would be unworthy of a benevolent Creator. A chunk of granite doesn't care if it's locked into static granitehood. But a human is a creature with a notable craving for self-determination. A divine plan that renders self-determination impossible makes that craving absurd and cruel. So either God doesn't exist, or God fumbled the ball and doesn't deserve our fidelity.[3]

Influential as it's been, I'm not too impressed by Sartre's argument. It's not at all obvious to me that a divinely pre-set human nature is as incompatible with human freedom as he thinks. (For example, if God "programmed" us to be rational, is that really an assault against free will? Most of us think that it's precisely rationality that enables us to will freely and wisely.) But Sartre's worry that the existence of God traps us between God walls and stifles our freedom is also the fundamental fear that drives Designerists to their god. They suffer from the opposite fear that haunts Church god devotees. They're afflicted with spiritual claustrophobia and believe that the existence of any deity other than Designer god inhibits their freedom, narrows their horizon, and bruises their individuality. Some of them come to this decision in wounded reaction to being on the receiving end of the harsh judgmentalism of Big Brotherites, the dogmatism of churcholaters, the intolerance of By the Bookers, or the bigotry of *My* godders. Others reach it because by temperament they're free spirits who have a hard time accepting any authority but their own. And still other Designerists are fashionistas who follow whatever the latest spiritual and theological trends happen to be.

Despite their shared claustrophobia, there's a significant difference between Sartre and Designerists. His bugaboo is a pre-set *human* nature. Theirs is a pre-set *divine* nature. Designerists are repulsed by the notion of a deity who doesn't bend to accommodate what they want in a god and who expects certain things from them regardless of their own inclinations. Their ideal is a pliable god who possesses whatever qualities they want him to have, not one whose unchanging

---

[3] Sartre defends this argument in several texts, but one of the more user-friendly ones is his short book *Existentialism Is a Humanism* (1946).

nature resists their attempts to redesign him or who makes moral and intellectual demands upon them. It's the deity, not them, who must make concessions. Otherwise, they feel stifled, pent up in a cell, and unable to spread their wings.

Worship of Designer god demolishes these God walls. Because he's accommodating enough to become whatever his devotees want him to be, he never gets in their way. Granted, he may wind up boring them after a period of time. Designerists tend to have short attention spans when it comes to the divine. But that's okay, because they can always redress the god mannequin in a more interesting getup. Mixing and matching is a favorite Designerist pastime.

I know someone who's a dedicated practitioner of this mix-and-match approach. She started out as a believer in a very orthodox Christian God, but soon decided that the moral dos and don'ts her Big Brotherite denomination associated with that God were too restrictive. So her deity morphed into a quasi-Taoist First Cause that created the universe but then stepped back to let everything run according to the Way or the Tao. Even though this new version conveniently placed no moral strictures upon her, she quickly decided that it was too impersonal for her taste. So she got out her shears, needle, and thread and stitched together a new god that was an amalgamation of Taoism and the old Christian God, but one that indulgently endorsed anything she wanted to do. This latest incarnation of Designer god suited her well enough for a while, but she eventually got a little bored with it and her god morphed yet again. Currently, she has a shrine in her apartment on which sits a statue of the Buddha, a Russian Orthodox icon of the Virgin Mary, a pebble that she brought back from a visit to Stonehenge, and a feather that symbolizes her latest god-interest, Wankan Tanka, the Great Spirit of the Sioux.

Can a person who belongs to a specific religious tradition find her spiritual life enriched by insights and practices from other ones? Absolutely. It's both arrogant and foolish to deny the possibility of fruitful cross-pollination. But a willingness to be stretched by different perspectives about God isn't the indiscriminate eclecticism embraced by Designerists. They're not interested in a deeper, richer, and potentially riskier relationship with God. They simply want a loose-fitting and flexible god robe that won't cramp or restrain them in the slightest way. A coat of many colors is just what the doctor (or shaman, guru, or latest New Age self-help author) ordered.

Designerists worship the god they do because the panic created by their spiritual claustrophobia blinds them to what freedom actually is. Contrary to what they think, freedom isn't an absolute absence of limitation or constraint. If it were, we'd have to say, ridiculously, that our inability to sprout wings and fly makes us unfree. Nor is freedom the same as doing or believing whatever we wish. The first is license, and the second fancy. Genuine freedom is the capacity to appraise an actual situation and then to make rational decisions unsullied by wishful thinking or unrealistic desires. Freedom recognizes that choices are always made in a context bound by the rules of rationality on the one hand and facts on the other. To defy gravity by jumping off a cliff and flapping one's arms isn't an exercise in freedom. It's foolishness or delusion, and it enslaves (or in this case, kills) rather than liberates. To attribute to a god whatever qualities we want him to possess, even when they're inconsistent with one another or go against everything we know about the world, is likewise foolish or delusional. It's a smashing of reality walls, not God walls. And how could that possibly be liberating?

Fragiles, free spirits, and *fashionistas*

All Designerists suffer from spiritual claustrophobia, but as we've seen, they deal with it in different ways. Some of them have been so traumatized that they're unable to place trust in anyone else's god, some are too free-spirited to bend the knee to a god not of their own making, and others are faddists who follow the latest trends.

The first group, the Fragiles, is a truly tragic one. Its members have been abused by others either in the name of religion or under the auspices of religion. The mistreatment can take any number of forms: spiritual bullying, joyless puritanism, dogmatic censure, oppressive watchdogging, shackling of the intellect, or, as we've witnessed all too often in recent years, sexual and emotional molestation. The ill-usage can be horrific or simply distasteful, episodic or chronic. But regardless of its form or frequency, it becomes inseparably associated in victims' minds with the god worshiped by their abusers—the god who, after all, condones, commands, or at the least turns a blind eye to the abuse.

There's a disturbing similarity in the behavior of Fragiles and abused spouses. Members of either group often remain in their abusive situations, sometimes leaving for short periods but eventually returning because their self-esteem has been so shattered that they believe themselves to blame for their ill treatment. The abused spouse tells herself she deserved the latest knocking-about because she mouthed off to her husband after he came home from a long night of drinking in a testy mood. The Fragile tells himself that he's a sinner corrupted by weak faith, willfulness, disrespect for religious elders or pride. Regardless of the specifics, it's he and not his religion that's the epicenter of trouble. Chances are, the longer he stays, the more his self-recrimination grows.

But of course not all victims of ill treatment stay. Some Fragiles, just like some abused spouses, do manage to make a break. A woman who escapes an abusive partner may swear off men for good because of the trauma she endured at the hands of one, or she may eventually venture another relationship with a male. But if she does, her very predictable impulse will be to fear and avoid men temperamentally similar to the one who abused her. Likewise, a Fragile's trauma may drive him to swear off all religion and to embrace disbelief. But even if he doesn't, his ill treatment leaves him with a strong aversion to being told by others what he should believe about God and how he should comport himself to please God. Hyper-sensitive to the presence of religious bullies and dogmatists, he backs away from them all, regardless of their religious affiliations, telling himself he wants nothing to do with any deity who sanctions their beliefs or their behavior. He protects himself by designing his own deity who, regardless of what other divine qualities he might have, keeps the gods of religious abusers at arm's length.

A Free Spirit hasn't been victimized like a Fragile, although she too feels stymied when others try to tell her she ought to believe this or that about God. A genuine individualist who bucks authority of any kind, disposed by both temperament and principle to be her own person, she prides herself on walking to the beat of a different drum. Sacred cows stick in her craw.

For a Free Spirit, conformity to conventions from any walk of life is a soul-imprisoning capitulation to the crowd. Near the top of her list of conventions to be avoided is any creed that an organized religion requires of its believers. She sees such things as top-down impositions. So she renounces conventional religiosity, and when and if she actually attends a mainstream church service, she does so either puckishly or rebelliously. A Free-Spirited friend of mine who occasionally comes to mass rewords the Nicene Creed during its corporate recitation to reject the bits she dislikes and to tack on others of her own invention. She comes to church because she has friends in the congregation and because, as she says, she likes the "smells and bells." But she doesn't for a moment kowtow to religious convention or churchly authority.

An expression frequently heard these days is, "I'm spiritual but not religious." It could easily be the rallying cry of Free Spirits (if, that is, they allowed themselves to be rallied, an unlikely possibility). They embrace the spiritual and deplore the religious. *Spiritual*, for them, is a looser, more liberating term than *religious,* which smacks of handed-down creeds and dogmas. As they see it, a "religious" approach focuses on uniformity of belief, conformity to rules, and an eye-popping list of prohibitions. A "spiritual" one, on the other hand, emphasizes the personal experience of finding one's own truth and trusting one's intuitions enough to take them as moral guides. A "religious" person is tied to the deity worshiped by his ancestors and proclaimed by his church. A "spiritual" person, recognizing that God is too big to fit into any one religious tradition, is free to design an eclectic deity and create her own tradition. And because she's its originator, she can also modify it at any time and in whatever way she wishes.

Fashionistas don't allow themselves quite as much freedom as Free Spirits when it comes to designing god. For the most part, they're trend followers rather than setters. Like weathercocks, they turn in the direction of the latest spiritual or religious or theological wind. Some—divinity students come to mind—can be quite sophisticated in their chase after the latest god-fashion, scrupulously redesigning their deity as many times as it takes to keep up with cutting-edge speculation. They also devour the latest scientific discoveries in physics and cosmology, just in case they offer some new tidbits about the Divine. Less sophisticated *fashionistas* enthusiastically embrace the latest cult or jump on the most recent religious bandwagon. Unsurprisingly, their worship is often inspired by their favorite celebrities. Popular interest in Hindu spirituality spiked in the late 1960s after the Beatles' George Harrison embraced Krishna Consciousness. Madonna's more recent infatuation with a New Age version of Kabbalah sparked her fans' interest in it. One of my students was drawn to Roman Catholicism because he admired Martin Sheen's performance as President Josiah Bartlet in *The West Wing*. Sheen is a Catholic, and so was the character he portrayed.

A distinctive feature of *fashionistas* is that they refuse to tie themselves down to any single god lest they miss the newer insight, the more fulfilling glimpse, the more accurate understanding of the deity that they're confident is just around the corner. They want to make sure that enough room is left in their "god closet" to fit in new accessories as they emerge. Whether it's the proclamation made by the latest hip prophet or the most recent dry-as-dust and nearly incomprehensible tome written by an academic theologian, they eagerly lap it up so as not to be embarrassingly behind the times in their thinking about the deity. Unfortunately, *fashionistas*, even the more sophisticated ones, tend not to be overly discriminating when it comes to quality. Their primary concern is to follow the mod crowd they want to be seen associating with or to emulate those celebrities whose gods seem to be the newest, coolest, and most exotic. They often wind up with trunk loads of out of fashion and boring god clothes. They pack them off to the attic, although they just might hang on to one or two items. You never know: the retro look could top the season one day, and a good *fashionista* wants to be prepared.

Buried in snow

All devotees of Designer god have this in common: they refuse to be tied down by convention or tradition. For Fragiles and Free Spirits, any ready-made deity that they've had no hand in constructing is too threatening, on the one hand, and too restrictive, on the other. *Fashionistas* eagerly await the thrill of each new season of god clothes. Above all, Designerists of any kind want a god that won't provoke their spiritual claustrophobia. They want to be unhindered.

As we've seen, though, Designerists fundamentally misunderstand what freedom is. They think it's the same as being totally rid of restriction. But if this is what freedom is, none of us possesses it because all of us are inevitably in specific situations and therefore limited by certain boundaries. This is simply the human condition. We are free rationally and realistically to make choices within those boundaries but not to step outside of them.

Genuinely exercising one's freedom, given its inevitably situated context, demands that we accept that some things are within our control and some things aren't. These latter are the givens of existence, and they must be acknowledged without self-delusion or denial if we wish to be free. One of the givens about God is that God is independent of us. We may, of course, choose to disbelieve in God. But if we *do* believe, we must accept as a religious given that God has a nature independent of whatever we might wish God to be. Otherwise, the word *God* is sapped of any intrinsic meaning, giving us license to begin inventing divine qualities that suit our fancy. The Do-It-Yourself Deity game becomes a way of life.

If this happens, we've fallen into the delusion of "snowflaking." In one of his best books, C. S. Lewis reflects on how easily we distort our mental images of acquaintances and even loved ones, dead as well as living, by remaking them the way we want them to be rather than the way they truly are.[4] We slowly and incrementally cover our memories or ideas of them with the "snow" of our own contrived impressions until eventually the real persons disappear. Lewis argues that one momentary encounter with them (if they're still living, that is) is often enough to sweep away the snowdrift. Our fancies, he believes, have very little resilience when they encounter the hard edge of reality. But I wonder if he underestimates how obstinate our self-deceptions can be. Snowbanks harden the longer they sit in place. The higher they pile up, the more difficult it is to shovel them away.

This is particularly true if we have a compelling interest in *not* clearing them. In the case of Designerists, their various strategies for snowflaking God into Designer god are defense mechanisms against spiritual claustrophobia. So naturally, they resist cranking up the spiritual snow blower. Fragiles bury any image of God except ones they design for themselves because their wounds make them neurotically risk aversive. Free Spirits snowflake any god that doesn't suit their personal

---

[4] C. S. Lewis explores snowflaking in *A Grief Observed* (1961). The book was written in an effort to cope with the death of his wife, Joy Davidman. In my opinion, Lewis wrote nothing better.

taste because they're afraid to face the possibility that their taste may be too limited or unrefined to be a reliable barometer of truth. *Fashionistas* throw themselves into the thick of whatever the latest snowfall brings.

Yet deny it as much as Designerists will, if there is a God, then God remains who God is. God is the ultimate given, the irreducible reality, the unchanging boundary that encompasses all of our situations. We can, hopefully, progress in our understanding of who and what God is, at least up to a certain point. But if God is real, it's as foolish to presume that God is whatever we wish God to be as it is to presume that Uncle Harry, if he's also real, can be whatever we want *him* to be. If wishes were horses, beggars would ride.

Chapter 10

Sunday School god

Think what a better world it would be if we all—the whole world—had cookies and milk about three o'clock every afternoon and then lay down with our blankies for a nap.

ROBERT FULGHUM[1]

When I was a child, I spoke like a child, I thought like a child, I reasoned like a child; when I became an adult, I put an end to childish ways.

—1 CORINTHIANS 13:11

In 1988, author Robert Fulghum became an overnight sensation by telling us that all we really need to know we learned in kindergarten. But with all due respect, this just isn't true. Kindergarten is for preschoolers, not adults.

To be fair to Fulghum, he *did* say that the lessons learned in kindergarten—share everything, play fair, don't hit other kids, say you're sorry when you hurt someone, flush, wash

---

[1] Robert Fulghum, *All I Really Need to Know I Learned in Kindergarten,* 15th ed. (New York: Ballantine, 2004), 3.

your hands—are elementary ones. But he insisted that they're
not simple, containing as they do rock-bottom wisdom that
can be applied to adult life. "Everything you need to know is
in there somewhere," he wrote. "The Golden Rule and love
and basic sanitation. Ecology and politics and equality and
sane living."[2]

The problem is that the moral and behavioral one-liners
taught in kindergarten portray the world in starkly one-
dimensional terms because those are the only ones a three- or
four-year-old kid can comprehend. It takes a few more years
under one's belt before the complexity of the world, human
relationships, and morality begins to sink in. Even after a full
lifetime, most of us go to our graves still trying to figure it all
out. In kindergarten it's good to share toys. But what does
"share everything" signify in an adult world divided into developed and developing nations? "Play fair" is another good
kindergarten lesson. It means something like "treat everybody
the same." But aren't there times in adult life when treating
people equally isn't the morally best thing to do? It's good
for young kids to get into the habit of washing their hands.
But what light does this bit of "sandpit wisdom," as Fulghum
calls it, shine on what we should do when it comes to global
pollution? Almost nothing we need to know to behave as
responsible adults is learned in kindergarten. Wisdom comes
from experience, reflection, and an appreciation of the world's
complexity. It doesn't come from naps, milk, and cookies.

I bring this up because there's a kind of idolatry that's the
religious analogue of Fulghum's kindergarten wisdom. Its
devotees believe that all they really need to know about God
they learned as children. Their deity is Sunday School god,
the benign old man in the sky—or, alternatively, the gentle-
eyed blondish Jesus or the sweetly dove-ish Holy Spirit—they
learned about and colored pictures of in church school. For
Sunday Schoolers, there's no mystery to be worried about, no
dark nights of the soul, no questions to be asked, no trembling

[2] Ibid., 5.

and awe to be experienced. God is exactly and only what they learned about God as kids. He's got the whole world in his hands. Jesus loves the little children, all the children of the world. If you love him and you know it, clap your hands *(clap clap clap!)*. Loving God makes you outright, upright, downright happy all the time. What else does anyone need to know?

Lost in Neverland

But wait a minute. What's so idolatrous about all this? Isn't it true that simplicity of faith is a virtue? Didn't Jesus himself say that we must be like little children to enter the kingdom?

When it comes to faith, there's a big difference—an unbridgeable one, in fact—between childlike simplicity and childishness. The first is a virtue, an innocent but not gullible trust in the essential goodness of God and the nobility of fellow humans. The second is an arrested-development way of thinking about God that never advances beyond the simplistic images and stories of Sunday School. I'll return to childlikeness at the end of this chapter. For now, let's explore the childishness that lies behind the worship of Sunday School god.

In 1984, Dr. Dan Kiley coined the expression *Peter Pan syndrome* to name the avoidance of adult responsibility he observed in many of his male patients.[3] Their overriding need for lifelong mothering kept them in such states of emotional, intellectual, and behavioral immaturity that sustaining healthy relationships with women was nearly off their radars. Since Kiley's time, psychologists have noted that women can suffer from Peter Pan syndrome as well. Their lifelong need for fathering inhibits them from developing an adult sense of responsibility, which in turn damages their ability to bond in rewarding ways with men.

---

[3] Dan Kiley, *The Peter Pan Syndrome: Men Who Have Never Grown Up* (London: Corgi, 1984).

Kiley named this tendency to self-infantilize after the well-known fictional character created by J. M. Barrie. Peter Pan is a youth who obstinately refuses to become an adult. He lives in a magical place called Neverland, which offers opportunities for any number of exciting adventures without any real dangers or grownup consequences. He eats when, where, and what he wishes, sleeps when he wishes, and in general leads an unstructured life unbounded by any rules or regulations except the ones that Wendy, his surrogate mother, tries to impose. At times he's so puzzled by the adult world that he feels out of sorts and melancholy. It never occurs to him that some of his bewilderment and sadness just might come from the fact that childhood oppresses when it ceases to be a developmental stage and becomes a permanent state.

Sunday Schoolers suffer from the spiritual version of Peter Pan Syndrome. They're child-men and child-women, stuck in pre-adolescence when it comes to thinking about God, even though they may be perfectly mature in other walks of life. Their Neverland, like Peter Pan's, is one where time has stopped. God remains always and forever the way he was portrayed in Sunday School. Just as they never grow up, neither does their god.

Barrie's Peter Pan remains a child because he's frightened of taking on adulthood responsibilities. What if he should fail?! Sunday Schoolers stay children because they're afraid of thinking about and relating to God in adult ways. What if doing so should complicate their lives?! So they're uncomfortable around and suspicious of those who disagree with their childish notion of God, and they go out of their way to avoid them. An acquaintance of mine once purchased a biography of Jesus written by a prominent British author. She had every reason to suspect that the biography would be properly pious; the author had a reputation as a Christian writer. But unknown to my acquaintance, the author had recently lost his faith (he's since recovered it), a change of circumstance that became obvious to readers after just a few pages. As soon as my acquaintance sensed the way the wind was blowing, she slammed the book shut. In telling me about the experience, she confessed that she probably would never open it again. "I'm afraid of it," she said. "I'm afraid it might weaken my faith." It's not for me to say if my acquaintance is a devotee of Sunday School god. But it *is* the case that the primary fear that motivates Sunday Schoolers is not unlike hers: a dread of their uncomplicated faith being challenged in the slightest way.

The fear that motivates Sunday Schoolers is double whammied. In the first place, they sense at some deep even if unarticulated level that their faith just might have its foundations in a sandbox instead of a rock, and this is an anxiety-generating sore spot. Why, otherwise, would even mild challenges threaten them so badly that they retreat into Neverland? Even child-adults must sometimes suspect, even if only vaguely, their immaturity. But they're simply not strong enough to resist the fear of growing up and facing the fact that while they've remained spiritually frozen in time, God, so to speak, has moved on.

In the second place, Sunday Schoolers are frightened of moving beyond their pre-adolescent understanding of the deity because the god they worship serves the same function for them that Wendy did for Peter Pan. Sunday School god mothers them, is forever there for them, always coddles them, never judges or rebukes them, never fails to tuck them safely into bed each night, and never taxes their brains. Because their god is forever the capable babysitter who serves as the responsible adult in their lives, they can excuse themselves from the task of thinking like adults about spiritual matters. To paraphrase Saint Paul, they continue eating crackerjacks and candy long after they should've switched over to nourishing adult food, and as a consequence they stunt their spiritual growth.

The kiddie food Sunday Schoolers like to munch on is served up to them by authority figures to whom they look for spiritual guidance—generally clergy who encourage their spiritual childishness by slapping an official seal of approval on it. Priests and pastors do this by treating and teaching their congregations as if they were made up of naive and easily frightened children. This clerical paternalism is sometimes ill intentioned. It's alarmingly easy for a minister trained in abstruse theology to fall into a slightly disdainful attitude toward parishioners and to get into the habit of deliberately talking down to them in sermons. But usually the paternalism is a well-intended but misguided effort to make parishioners' faith journeys comfortable by feeding them simple, entertaining, and unthreateningly familiar narratives. Children never get tired of hearing the same bedtime stories over and over and over again. But there comes a point in their development when they need to move on to other kinds of literature that stretch their imaginations and their reason.

Congregations are infantilized and Sunday School god idolatry is encouraged when sermonizing clergy speak of God in overly anthropomorphic ways and read scripture too literally; when they sideline those parts of the Bible that are either perplexing or troubling (for example, the Old Testament "terrible texts" in which God seems to applaud wholesale slaughter); when they refuse to incorporate challenging but potentially enriching theological insights into their sermons and counseling; when they oversimplify the complexity of most moral dilemmas; and when they carefully steer their people away from art, books, or films that might suggest that God is more complicated than what gets taught in Sunday School. I fully appreciate how difficult it is for clergy and other religious authorities to resist feeding their people unhealthy junk food and instead serve up nutritious but sometimes hard-to-chew fare. It requires finesse, experience, faith, courage, and good will to avoid nurturing Peter Pans, and doing so almost inevitably means that once in a while a Sunday Schooler in the congregation will become upset or even temporarily traumatized. But helicopter clergy who hover over their parishioners to make sure that they never hear anything that might spiritually distress them wind up encouraging their spiritual underdevelopment, just as helicopter parents put their kids at risk of becoming child-adults.

Tortilla Jesus

In 1977, as she rolled a tortilla for her husband, Eduardo's, breakfast, Maria Rubio noticed a small, thumb-sized burn that looked, she decided, like the face and shoulders of Jesus.[4] By that afternoon all her neighbors in the small New Mexico town of Lake Arthur had dropped by to see and marvel at the miracle. Before long, Maria quit her job as a maid to dedicate herself to the stream of visitors who came to see and venerate the tortilla apparition; by 1979 there had been over thirty-five thousand pilgrims. Maria eventually had a small shed built in her back yard, and inside it she enshrined the miraculous tortilla in a glass case, visible to the many pilgrims who left written prayers for healing, financial success, conception, and so on. The shrine is now closed, after the tortilla was accidentally broken.

Maria's miraculous tortilla isn't in a class of its own. Hardly a month goes by without another sighting of Jesus or the Virgin Mary in a piece of toast, a rusted screen, a gnarled tree trunk, or a grilled cheese sandwich. (These are all actual examples, by the way.) As soon as news of each new apparition spreads, hundreds flock to see it, some of them traveling extraordinary distances. Roman Catholic authorities are extremely wary of such sightings, being perfectly aware of a psychological tendency called pareidolia, which prompts humans to "see" or "discover" meaning in random and vague stimuli. The man in the moon is an obvious example of pareidoliac perception, as is the spotting of animals, ships, and human faces in cloud formations. Chances are good that the sightings of Jesus in tortillas and other unlikely objects are as well.

Sunday Schoolers live for these starkly concrete confirmations of their god. It never strikes them as odd that God would choose to imprint his image on a tortilla, or that there's something just a little suspect about automatically assuming that the

---

[4] For a profile and history of Maria Rubio's discovery, see "Shrine of the Miracle Tortilla," available on the RoadsideAmerica.com website.

image looks just like Jesus as opposed to any other bearded man. After all, no one knows what Jesus actually looked like. But that's no problem for Sunday Schoolers, because they think of God in very specific and well-defined anthropomorphic terms: masculine, bearded, and robed, something straight off the Sistine Chapel ceiling. For them, as for *My* godders, calling God *personal* means that God *is* a person—although somehow not a mortal one—who lives in a heaven that's literally *up* there somewhere in the sky. Metaphors, similes, analogies, and poetic attempts to express the Divine are all taken literally by Sunday Schoolers. It's not necessarily because they also have By the Book tendencies, although they may, but because they refuse to progress beyond a pre-adolescent notion of who and what God is. They're stuck in a spiritual developmental stage that psychologist James Fowler, who specializes in religious development, calls "mythic-literal."

According to Fowler, the mythic-literal stage of faith is typical of seven- to twelve-year-olds. When it comes to thinking about God, the reference points of this stage are the detailed "factual" descriptions found in Bible stories and narratives. What spiritually mature adults consider to be mythic or symbolic in these descriptions, the child takes literally. If God is described as "walking in the garden at the time of the evening breeze" (Gen 3:8), children believe it to mean exactly what it says. Likewise, they hear Jesus's parables primarily as descriptions of events that actually happened, and only secondarily, if at all, as literary devices intended to point beyond themselves toward moral or spiritual points. Children in the mythic-literal developmental stage are unable, observes Fowler, to "step back from stories, reflect upon them, and . . . communicate their meanings by way of more abstract and general statements."[5] They simply haven't developed the cognitive skills to perform such operations.

---

[5] James Fowler, *Stages of Faith: The Psychology of Human Development and the Quest for Meaning* (New York: HarperOne, 1995), 136–37.

Sunday School god devotees have reached a chronological age where they should be able to think less literally about God while still appreciating the rich imagery of traditional narratives. But for one reason or another they have remained at the mythic-literal level. As spiritual Peter Pans, they focus on the particular details of the stories to the exclusion of grownup analysis of them. Their fixation on concrete narrative is what attracts them to reports of Jesus and Mary apparitions, however incredible they may be. Visual manifestations of God, even on slices of toast, are entirely plausible to them because the only kind of deity they can imagine is the very concrete one whom their Sunday School taught them about—the god, as the old hymn has it, who walks with them, and talks with them, and who tells them they're never alone. Sunday Schoolers take this kind of imagery at face value.

Elementary school kids and adult Sunday Schoolers share another characteristic when it comes to thinking about spiritual matters. Their view of the moral order is as black and white as their interpretation of biblical narratives is literal. They believe there's a principle of perfectly proportioned normative give-and-take at play in the universe. If they only follow all the rules (share everything, play fair, and flush, as Fulghum might say), they'll inevitably receive divine rewards; if not, divine punishment. Fowler interviewed one adult woman, for example, who told him that she prays on a regular basis so that "when I need it, it's in the bank." For her, Fowler concluded, the purpose of prayer was "to store up God's good favor against times when special help or forgiveness" would be needed. This is typical of the way Sunday Schoolers reduce normative complexity to simplistic recipes, and it parallels their one-dimensional understanding of God.[6]

The research of Gordon Allport, another psychologist who focuses on religious development, sheds additional light on the spirituality of Sunday School god devotees. He argues that immature religious perspectives in adults are characterized by

---

[6] Ibid., 147, 148.

several discernible characteristics. Adults who fail or refuse to grow up spiritually, for example, typically indulge in a lot of magical thinking that predisposes them to high levels of credulity. They believe unquestioningly that Jesus appears in tortillas and that when he does, he can be petitioned and implored for boons.

Not surprisingly, Allport also discovered that Sunday Schoolers are remarkably unreflective when it comes to their religious beliefs. They hold them with such certainty and have such effective screening mechanisms against challenges, that the need to think about them, much less critically examine them, is rarely felt. Their lack of religious reflection means that they rarely reflect or read religious books. As a consequence, they get nearly everything they believe about God from Sunday School classes, sermons, and one-on-one conversations with ministers—a fact that underscores the danger of helicopter clergy encouraging spiritual Peter Panism.

An especially disturbing characteristic of Sunday School god devotees noticed by Allport is that they, like pre-adolescent children, tend to be profoundly gullible when it comes to religious matters. They readily swallow the most incredible stories just so long as they're told by people they trust. Their tendency to think in one-dimensional terms and their ensuing lack of discrimination makes them particularly receptive, and susceptible, to charismatic religious leaders, just as children are entranced by good storytellers.[7]

Think of the extraordinary hold that televangelists, high priests of spiritual Peter Panism, have on Sunday Schoolers. Whether they're honest or bamboozlers or a little of both, most televangelists preach a simplistic faith that reflective Christians find implausible. It doesn't matter if it's the gospel of wealth, speaking in tongues, miraculous healing, or fundamentalist preaching. The message is especially designed to evaporate the mystery of God and reassuringly reduce

---

[7] For Allport's study of religious development, see Gordon Willard Allport, *The Individual and His Religion* (New York: Macmillan, 1967).

complex matters of faith to a handful of one-liners. Gullible Sunday School followers hang on every word, defend them fiercely, remain loyal to them even after scandal strikes (as it often does), and regularly throw millions of dollars in their direction to support their so-called ministries. One of the crueler jokes Sunday School god plays on his devotees is putting them in the hands of these Pied Pipers.

Childlikeness

I mentioned at the beginning of this chapter that there's a profound difference between the spiritual childishness of a Sunday School god worshiper and the childlikeness recommended by Jesus. We've examined the first. Now it's time to explore the second.

Two literary portraits of spiritual childlikeness come immediately to mind, both of them from Dostoyevsky. One is Prince Myshkin from *The Idiot* and the other is Alyosha from *The Brothers Karamazov*. Myshkin is a loving and otherworldly soul whose simple goodness both bewilders and intrigues the jaded jet set of St. Petersburg. Alyosha, one of the Karamazov boys, is a youth whose sensitivity especially attunes him to both the joys of life and the suffering that so many unfortunate people endure.

At first glance, both Myshkin and Alyosha come across as dopes or "idiots" who are too simple-minded to survive in the real world. They trust people as unreservedly as they love God. They seem ripe for the plucking by even a modestly talented con artist.

But the reader quickly discovers that Myshkin and Alyosha are anything but babes in the wood. They both clearly recognize evil when they're confronted by it. Their innocence isn't a moral blindness but rather a refusal to judge and condemn others. They refuse to judge because their default position is openness to the possibility of goodness in each person they encounter. This is quite different from the blind gullibility of Sunday Schoolers, who see the moral order in exclusively black and white terms. It's certainly true that their trusting openness, their childlike willingness to be fully present to others, uninhibited by preconceptions or prejudices, makes Myshkin and Alyosha vulnerable. But this trustful vulnerability is also what attracts and inspires many of the people who meet them.

Dostoyevsky clearly modeled both of his characters on the Russian Orthodox tradition of the holy fool or *yurodivy*. A holy fool is a man or woman so focused on God that he or she ignores social conventions and norms, and thus appears mad or fanatical or childish to the rest of us. Holy fools have been known, for example, to walk around Moscow naked, even in the wintertime. Sometimes they wander the countryside; sometimes they live in hovels in cities. They can remain silent for years on end and then erupt in public lamentations over the excesses of princes and czars. They are genuine innocents, in the sense that they neither understand nor value what the rest of society holds dear or even sacred. They are childlike in their lack of interest in worldly success, reputation, and power. Yet they're anything but childish. Their faith in God is profound and ever present, but they don't for a moment presume that God is a bearded man in the sky. They may be foolish in the eyes of the world, but they're neither unreflective nor literal minded. And above all, they're unafraid.

So a childlike spirituality has nothing in common with the childish one embraced by Sunday Schoolers. But at the same time, childlikeness doesn't belong only to holy fools like Prince Myshkin and Alyosha. If it did, most of us would be in trouble, because we're simply not in their spiritual league. Their kind of innocence is a charism unshared by most. But this doesn't mean that the childlike trust and nonjudgmentalism recommended by Jesus and practiced by holy fools is totally beyond our reach. To the extent that we cultivate it, we help immunize ourselves against the infection of Sunday School idolatry.

Philosopher and theologian Paul Ricoeur calls the child-likeness that's open to all of us a "second naivete," as distinguished from "first naivete," the wide-eyed gullibility with which we swallowed everything we were told as children, an unreflective acceptance at face value of any religious story we were told. First naivete is the way of responding to the world characteristic of Fowler's mythic-literal stage of faith development.

For most of us the development of cognitive skills and greater exposure to the world create a critical distance or gap between us and the religious beliefs we accepted as kids. It becomes increasingly difficult to square a literal reading of every line in scripture with what we know about the world, just as it becomes inconceivable that God is a bearded and robed man who lives in the sky. Reason, in other words, prompts us to take a step back from our childishly naive beliefs so that we gain the distance or perspective required for a critical examination of them. When we do, we see that many of them simply don't hold up.

At this point readers might conclude that Ricoeur means to defend a rational jettisoning of faith. But nothing is further from his intent. He argues that the critical distancing that sweeps away first-naivete beliefs needn't spell an end to faith but can actually open the door to a more mature and rich one. Reason, he believes, liberates us from childishness and prepares us for childlikeness. Loss of faith, if it occurs, is often only a prelude to entry into the second naivete, in which we return to the stories and narratives that we accepted at face value before we reached the age of reason and discover that even though they're not literally plausible, they do possess great spiritual significance. God may not be a bearded old man in the sky, but the image is a powerful archetype that symbolizes wisdom and transcendence. Jesus may or may not have literally quelled a storm, but the story that describes him as doing so reminds us that he can calm our own troubled waters. The stories that lived for us when we accepted them as literal truth but seemed to die when scrutinized from a critical distance now reveal new and saving meaning. We accept them in good conscience as spiritually significant parables even as we reject them as literal descriptions. And the insight into God and human existence that they bring allows us once again to trust that there is deep meaning and purposefulness to the universe, even if a final understanding of it eludes us. We move from the childish faith of children to the childlike faith of spiritually healthy adults. We put away the comforting tangibles of childhood for the infinitely more rewarding complexities of adulthood.[8]

We should beware of Robert Fulghum's recommendation that warm milk and cookies followed by an afternoon nap is a cure for the world's problems. Even as a metaphor, this kind of advice is more cute than astute. It trivializes complexity, and it infantilizes adults. It's a bad way to dwell in the world. Similarly, we should beware of claims that everything we need to know about God we learned in Sunday School, and that overcomplicating those simple pearls of wisdom needlessly confuses us. We're all children of God, and most of us may be mere babes in the faith. But this doesn't mean that we need be child-adults.

---

[8] For a discussion of first and second naivete, see Paul Ricoeur, "Conclusion," *The Symbolism of Evil* (Boston: Beacon Press, 1967), 347–57.

Chapter 11

Egghead god

God of Abraham, God of Isaac, God of Jacob—not of the philosophers and scholars.

—Blaise Pascal

What the philosophers describe by the name of God cannot be more than an idea.

—Martin Buber[1]

When I was nineteen, something happened that, within five minutes, publicly humiliated me beyond anything I'd ever experienced before—or since, for that matter. For years I looked back on it as one of the worst moments of my life.

I was an undergraduate, majoring in philosophy. Like many philosophy students, I was passionately in love with ideas,

---

[1] Blaise Pascal, "Memorial," which was written in an effort to describe a mystical experience he had when he was thirty-one. Pascal apparently never told anyone about the experience. But it so moved him that he sewed the "Memorial" inside his coat, wearing it next to his heart for the rest of his life. It was only discovered after his death. For the quotation from Buber, see Martin Buber, *Eclipse of God* (Amherst, NY: Humanity Books, 1952), 49.

and once I started rattling on about the latest philosopher I'd discovered, my long-suffering family and friends found it hard to shut me up. I was intoxicated with ideas, seduced by theory. Nothing delighted me more than a well-hewn philosophical system. The more abstract it was, the more it appealed to me. I longed for The Grand Theory That Explains Everything Including God.

At the beginning of my junior year I received permission to enroll in a graduate seminar. A bit intimidated because I was the only undergraduate in it, I compensated by becoming one of those students whose hand is perpetually in the air, eager to share my nineteen-year-old wisdom with the prof and my classmates. I was forever spinning abstruse theories in class, ignoring the professor's attempts to bring me down to earth. But I was pretty disdainful of the world of mere facts. It was too messy for me, too booming and buzzing. I preferred the arctic cleanness of abstraction.

I must've been insufferable.

Now for the humiliating moment. It occurred right after one of my long-winded mini-lectures, volunteered in response to a question posed to the class by our professor. When I finally stopped talking, he stared at me for a few quiet seconds. I was pretty sure his silence was an awed homage to my brilliance and confidently awaited his praise. But what I got instead was this, said in a rather weary but not unkind way: "Mr. Walters, would you do something for us? I wonder if you'd come to the front of the room, climb up on this table, and repeat what you just said while hopping up and down on one leg and rubbing your belly."

There was dead silence in the room. Even those students who found me most annoying must've felt too embarrassed for me to snicker or applaud. I sat in my desk for the rest of the period, paralyzed with rage and shame, blushing furiously. When the class finally ended, I made a rush for the door, avoiding eye contact with everyone. The next morning I went straight to the registrar's office and dropped the course, and I went out of my way to avoid running into the offending professor during my remaining two years at university. I managed to pull that off. But the memory of his public humiliation of me stuck in my craw for the next ten years or so.

To this day I don't know if my professor's invitation was a thoughtful effort to rein me in—academic shock therapy, as it were—or if he simply ran out of patience with me and decided to give me my comeuppance. But although it took a few years, I gradually began to see it taught me a good lesson—two, in fact—that in my thick-headedness I might not have otherwise picked up. The first and more obvious one was not to take myself so seriously. The second, especially pertinent to the idolatry I want to explore in this chapter, was not to take theory and abstraction so seriously. The first was a lesson in personal humility; the second, a lesson in intellectual humility.

Seduced by abstraction

Intellectuals (and budding ones) are especially likely to fall into the trap of becoming so intrigued with their own pristinely laid-out conceptual frameworks that they prefer them to the more tropical world of everyday experience and empirical facts. This observation isn't meant to trash abstraction in even the slightest way. One of the most distinctive and essential human characteristics is the ability to think in this way. Alone of all creatures, we can move from a focus on the concrete here and now to conceive of generalities and patterns, infer future events, imagine alternatives, manipulate language, and evaluate options. Given the paucity of our survival-enhancing physical skills and strength, it's a toss up whether our species would've made it in the evolutionary scramble without our talent for abstraction. It's what enables the "higher-order" thinking of physicists and philosophers that often seems to have no immediate practical value. But the ability to abstract also invents the wheel, builds bridges, flies airplanes, and cures diseases. Abstraction is necessary for simply getting through the day.

That being said, it's also the case that higher-order abstractions can become so seductive that they, rather than the reality they're intended to understand, become the focus of attention. When I was a kid growing up on a farm, I used to watch my grandmother strain fresh cow milk through cheese cloth to catch impurities. Formal conceptual frameworks aim to help us nab impurities in our thinking about reality. We strain our experiences through them in the hope of separating true from false opinion. But if we're not careful, our conceptual straining can block too much, and then we're left with a pretty thin gruel for our efforts. For intellectuals who are bewildered and perhaps even a little repulsed by the actual world's thickness, this purging appeals. It serves up an orderly and rational alternative to everyday experience by focusing on a grid that transforms otherwise random, mysterious, or even chaotic events into sense-making features of a formal system. Natural laws, mathematical axioms, metaphysical systems, and logic are all attempts to understand specific events and entities by plugging them into abstract frameworks.

These frameworks not only speak to our human hunger for intelligibility. They also attract us by their beauty. Although they may not be everyone's cup of tea, there's an aesthetically pleasing symmetry and elegance to geometrical proofs, chemical formulas, or technical philosophical arguments. In his dialogue *Symposium*, Plato argued that the more abstract our thinking becomes, the more its beauty satisfies our reason. But of course conceptual order isn't attractive to just our reason. It also appeals to our senses. If you doubt this, reflect on the fact that most of us find ceramic tiles, paintings, or buildings decorated with nonrepresentational arabesques hauntingly lovely.

Moreover, abstraction and theory can seduce because they are our own offspring. They spring from our heads, and we take parental pride in them. Conceptualization is always creation, and it's easy for artists to become so enamored of their art that they forget it *is* art. Poor Pygmalion falling in love with his own sculpture: the myth is a warning against growing so fond of our own abstractions that we mistake them for the reality they try to represent.

Eggheadery

There's a species of idolatry especially appealing to anyone who feels the allure of formal conceptual systems. It venerates an utterly abstract deity who is the conclusion of a crisp syllogism or an elaborate theological argument. His devotees, generally people who are big in the brains department, sink so deeply into their abstract systems that they find it difficult to surface. Their temples are their own minds; their prayer books are theological and philosophical treatises. They stand on holy ground whenever they retreat from the confusing material world to roam the heavenly city of abstract thinking about divine matters. And enthroned at the center of that city is Egghead god, the Cosmic Equation that explains everything, the Unified Theory, the First Principle, the Grand Architect, the Unmoved Mover. If Eggheaders occasionally use personal pronouns to refer to their deity, it's more a matter of conventional habit than anything else. Personal pronouns don't really apply to Egghead god because he (or rather *it*) has all the personality of a mathematical equation. You can admire the god's stark conceptual simplicity (or complexity, depending on which abstract model you're working with). But you don't get intimate with him . . . um, it.

The existential inadequacy of this hyper-conceptual god has been noted time and again. Back in the seventeenth century, Blaise Pascal, one of his generation's towering intellects and apparently an Eggheader until a midlife mystical experience knocked him out of his idolatry, recommended the *living reality* of the God of Abraham, Isaac, and Jacob in contrast to the *ideas about God* favored by philosophers. Three centuries later Jewish mystic Martin Buber likewise warned against conflating a philosophical concept of God with God. And even Sigmund Freud, who had no use for gods of any kind, opined that although all believers are mistaken, philosophically oriented ones are especially so. "Philosophers stretch the meaning of words until they retain scarcely anything of their original sense," he wrote. "By calling 'God' some vague abstraction that they have created for themselves, they pose as believers before the world; they may even pride themselves on having attained a higher, purer idea of God, although their God is nothing but an insubstantial shadow and no longer the mighty personality of religious doctrine."[2]

If we take these observations seriously, are we obliged to conclude that even though abstraction and theory are essential in other fields of human inquiry, they're not when it comes to thinking about God? Or, even stronger, that they actually stand between God and us, erecting a conceptual wall that keeps us locked inside our pet theories about God? The answer, in a word, is no.

Short of a direct experience of God, all our thinking about him is inescapably abstract. The very word *God* is an abstraction, designating an often staggeringly complex set of theoretical assumptions about reality, values, human nature, and purposefulness. Moreover, any attempt to argue that we ought to cease thinking abstractly about God is literally self-refuting. There have been a few figures in the history of Western religion who claimed to renounce abstract thinking about God because they believed it got in the way of faith. But they didn't really, because one can't.[3]

What separates legitimate thinking about God from what Eggheaders do isn't the abstraction per se, then, but rather its motivation. A rational thinker hungers for a deeper understanding of God, even if pursuing it means that he has to

---

[2] Sigmund Freud, *The Future of an Illusion* (New York: W. W. Norton, 1975), 51.

[3] I'm thinking of so-called fideists such as Tertullian (third century), al-Ghazali (1058–1111), and Søren Kierkegaard (1813–55).

jettison many of his ideas and theories about God. He does so willingly, because he knows full well that the most intellectually sophisticated models in the world inevitably fall short of God, and he doesn't want to get trapped in them. But the Eggheader is so infatuated with his own thinking about God that he finds it excruciating to do much more than tinker around his theory's edges. He refuses to take counterarguments seriously, never lets facts get in the way of his model, and is usually disdainful of what he sees as muddle-headed folk religion. Its emotionalism looks dingy in contrast to the elegant purity of his conceptual framework. Hard and unsentimental thought: that's the proper offering to lay before Egghead god's altar.

But of course what the Eggheader means by "hard and unsentimental thought" at the end of the day applies only to his theoretical understanding of God. Earlier I referred to Pygmalion as the prototype of an Eggheader's tendency to become enamored of his own abstractions. Another figure from the classical tradition illustrates the Eggheader's blindness to any idea or experience that doesn't fit his conceptual model. I'm talking about Procrustes, the mythical innkeeper who thought it more convenient to force his guests to fit the sizes of his beds than the other way around. If a guest was too tall for the bed, Procrustes lopped off his legs; if too short, Procrustes stretched him. Inspired by this bizarre mode of hospitality, we now speak of a "procrustean theory" or a "procrustean analysis" to describe a conceptual framework (or "bed") that stretches or contracts annoyingly odd-shaped facts until they fit the model.

Eggheaders are dyed-in-the-wool procrusteans when it comes to God, possessively protecting their own abstract models against the encroachment of contrary evidence. Either they ignore it, or they stretch, shrink, or strain it to make it fit into their own frameworks. Devotees of Designer god take "stitch and sew" as their motto. "Cut 'em, stretch 'em, or strain 'em" is the Eggheader's mantra.

Fearing mystery, dodging commitment

Underneath the Eggheader's delight with her pristinely conceptual god is a species of the intellectual pride that made me such an annoying prig when I was at university. It's heady stuff, creating worlds with one's mind. It's even more of a thrill making God conform to a conceptual framework. When you think about it, it's a bit like being divine oneself.

But if we dig a bit deeper, we discover that Eggheadery is built only secondarily on intellectual pride and primarily, like any idolatry, on fear. Devotees of Egghead god are frightened of what the Catholic philosopher Gabriel Marcel called "mystery."

There are times when the world in which we dwell reveals itself, to use Marcel's term, as problematic. When we're confronted by a problem—a misplaced cell phone, a crossword puzzle, a vexing ache in the shoulder, or a birthday toy that needs assembling—we typically see it as an obstacle to be overcome by hard thinking. We may not be able to solve the problem right away. In fact, it may take years to work through it. But, by definition, all problems are solvable. The only questions they pose are answerable ones. There's nothing intrinsically unknowable about them. So, given enough time and enough data, we can crack any problem. The trick is to keep ourselves emotionally detached when tackling them to ensure objectivity and clarity. Even if it's a problem upon which a great deal is riding—the cure for AIDS or cancer, for example—maintaining an objective distance is a necessary condition for arriving at a solution. This is Science 101.

Objective problem solving has two other familiar characteristics. First, cracking a problem doesn't depend on any one person, because anyone trained in problem-solving skills can step in. Problem solvers, like machine parts, are interchangeable. Additionally, the objectivity that they bring to their work minimizes the chance of their being intimately affected by what they do. They may experience a sense of achievement when the problem gets fixed, and their success may even bring them rewards if the problem they cracked was an especially big one. But their inner being, their essential identity, isn't affected by slogging away at a problem. It stands apart from them, and they from it. Solving it is just a task, and when it's finished, they move on to the next problem.

So far, so good. The ability to discern and properly relate to the problematic is a must-have personal and social skill set. It's obviously at the heart of both the scientific method and technological research. But it's also necessary in everyday living. After all, problem solving is what enables us to find that misplaced cell phone.

There is, however, a second way in which the world reveals itself. Marcel calls it mystery. "A problem," he writes, "is something which I meet, which I find completely before me, [and] which I can therefore lay siege to and reduce." Mystery, on the other hand, "is something in which I am myself involved, and it can therefore only be thought of as a sphere where the distinction between what is in me and what is before me loses its meaning and initial validity."[4] Mystery can't be approached with the conceptual tools of abstract thought, calculation, and common sense we properly bring to problems. On the contrary, an experience of mystery dissolves the possibility of objective detachment requisite for problem solving. Problem solvers may be interchangeable, but an experience of mystery is irreducibly personal because my whole identity, not just my brain power, is called forth. An experience of mystery involves my very being. When I encounter it, abstraction gives way to embodied awe, to a *frisson* of surprise or anticipation, and to the recognition that decision, not inspection, is necessary. I question a problem, but mystery questions me. Problems elicit scrutiny; mystery elicits response. How oxygen bonds with nitrogen is a

---

[4] Gabriel Marcel, *Being and Having* (Westminster, UK: Dacre Press, 1949), 117.

problem. Loving another human being is mystery. Drawing up architectural plans for a church, temple, or mosque is a problem. Experiencing the living God within the built sanctuary is mystery.

Marcel worries that we're losing touch with mystery. For the last two or so centuries, he argues, we've been so fixated on the problem-solving response to the world associated with the natural sciences that we've come to see it as the only legitimate kind. This, in turn, has nurtured the conviction that the world is nothing but a vast network of problems. Predictably, our sensitivity to mystery has coarsened. Human love became a problem to be unraveled by the behavioral and neurological sciences, and the experience of beauty by the psychology of perception. Truth got reduced to nothing more than a function of fact-describing propositions. And for the Eggheader, God became just another problem in a universe of problems, an object of inquiry to be abstractly scrutinized and strained through a theoretical framework. It's revealing that many theologians in the modern era refer to their discipline as the *science* of God.

But whatever else God may be, God certainly isn't a problem, in Marcel's sense of the word, to be solved. God is divine Mystery, to be experienced by us but not conquered by abstract thinking. Divine Mystery can be evoked in the language of poetry but not described in scientific terms. Encountering it reveals aspects of reality that simply can't be reduced to naturalistic explanations. When I encounter the mystery of God, it challenges me to a personal response. Do I open myself to it, or do I resist it? Do I accept divine Mystery's offer of deep even if ultimately unspeakable meaning, or do I flee it by trying to reduce it to the safely problematic? The experience of mystery is a question that invites me to take a leap of faith, and there's no cushion of objectivity, technique, and calculation to soften my landing.

Make no mistake about it: leaping into divine Mystery, allowing oneself to be pulled in by its invitation, takes courage, especially in a culture that continuously assures us that we're problem-solving masters of the universe. To run up against a God who refuses to be reduced to the problematic is a shock that can trigger a seismic shift in how we think of ourselves and the world. It rockets us away from abstract theorizing about God straight into the divine wind tunnel. Eggheaders simply can't bear the thought of being sucked through it toward a Mystery that can't be domesticated by conceptual frameworks. Getting that up close and personal calls for a level of humility and commitment they find both frightening and distasteful. So they dodge the divine Mystery and turn instead to the much more manageable god of logical theorems and byzantine theologies. Why risk the wind tunnel when you can hunch safely and snugly over computer keyboards and books? Why venture into the uncharted rainforest when you can harbor in the arctic of abstract formal systems?

Than which nothing more abstract can be thought

Perhaps a specific example of Eggheadery's transformation of divine Mystery into abstract problem would be helpful at this point.

Sometime in 1078, a Benedictine monk named Anselm wrote a short book—little more than a pamphlet, really—entitled *Proslogion*. The book isn't a philosophical treatise so much as an extended prayer for insight into God's nature. But embedded within it is a demonstration of the existence of God that has come to be known as the ontological argument (ontological simply refers to "being"). The argument has intrigued philosophers and theologians for an entire millennium, prompting thousands of responses. Many think that the argument is downright bogus, while others suspect that there's something wrong with it but can't quite figure out what. Still others conclude that the argument is either irrefutable as it stands or believe that it can be strengthened if reformulated into modal logic, a modern tool unavailable to Anselm. But whether critics accept or reject it, the ontological argument approaches God not as a mystery that calls for a response on our part but as a problem to be solved by dispassionate and rigorously abstract cogitation. I don't think this was Anselm's intention—his argument, after all, is part of a beautiful and obviously heartfelt prayer—but it's certainly the outcome. The deity he arrives at is as abstract as it gets. No wonder Egg-headers never tire of chewing on the ontological argument.

Anselm's demonstration runs like this. You and I can conceive of a being "than which nothing greater can be conceived," a being more real than anything else that is. But if this being is merely a concept—if it exists *only* in our minds—then even the lowliest thing that actually exists in the world has more reality, because physical objects are more real than mental ones. Therefore, a necessary feature of a being that is *truly* that "than which nothing greater can be conceived" is that it must actually exist, and this being we call "God."[5]

You can see why the argument has intrigued so many people. It's simple, it's elegant, and there's a head-spinning subtlety to it bound to attract anyone who likes working through puzzles and problems. But notice that even though the argument purports to be about God, in Anselm's hands the word *God* signifies an entity whose only pertinent quality, to be more real than anything else, is utterly abstract. It's an exclusively cerebral analysis of the meaning of the words *conceive, real, God,* and their logical relationship to one another. Once you grasp their meanings, says Anselm, you know that God exists. Problem solved.

Like all problems, the ontological argument requires absolutely no personal involvement or commitment on our part. All it demands is hard, abstract thinking, using the formal tools of logic and language analysis. An atheist can be just as intrigued by it as a theist. In fact, one of my friends, a

---

[5] Anselm, *Proslogion*, trans. Thomas Williams (Indianapolis, IN: Hackett, 2001). Williams's translation includes the response of Anselm's contemporary Gaunilo.

very good logician who's also a convinced atheist, has been obsessed with it for years. For any aficionado of abstract problem solving, the sheer intellectual excitement of wrestling with Anselm's argument can easily overshadow interest in whether there actually is a God. The thrill of the puzzle, the heady rush of cracking open an elaborate argument, takes center stage. It tickles the Eggheader's temperamental inclination to abstract thought; its reduction of divine Mystery to philosophical problem pumps up his intellectual pride; and it builds a firewall that protects him from an unsettling encounter with divine Mystery. The ontological argument is a great way to talk about God without actually running into him.

I wouldn't want to be misunderstood here. I'm not suggesting that Anselm or anyone who takes the ontological argument seriously is necessarily an idolater. Nor do I mean to imply that rigorous thinking about God is somehow in and of itself suspect. Such an implication is both mistaken and dangerous, opening the door to far worse alternatives like By the Book or Sunday School idolatry. But in the hands of an Eggheader, abstract theorizing about God gets fetishized as an end in itself.

Virtual god

The computer age has added dozens of new words to our lexicon that weren't needed by earlier generations: *download, upload, mainframe, gigabytes, mouse pad*. But there's at least one computer-age term that applies retroactively: *virtual reality*.

Today, the phrase signifies cyberspace images that provide us with experiences that simulate reality. By surfing the Internet we can take virtual tours of Greece and Turkey, sit in on virtual classrooms, or (most popular of all) have virtual sex. Because these virtual experiences are so available and so user friendly—after all, a virtual tourist doesn't have to put up with the hassles of real travel—many of us find ourselves actually preferring them to the real thing.

Even though computer-created virtual reality is a new phenomenon, virtual reality isn't. Eggheaders through the centuries have preferred their abstract models of God to God himself. As we've seen, this is partly because they fear the commitment that an experience of Mystery demands, and partly because birthing virtual gods feeds their intellectual pride. But as is the case with today's cyberspace virtual reality, part of the appeal of their abstract models is that they're clean and hassle free, enabling Eggheaders to bypass the risk of doubt, confusion, and occasional despair, all pretty predictable moments in any person's faith life.

But there's something about humans that ultimately can't be satisfied with formal reasoning and conceptual frameworks. We have a deep-seated craving for reality, even when reality's hard edge intimidates and maybe repels us. I suspect that even in Anselm's abstract argument, his definition of God as that which is most real is an expression of this craving. You and I may at times fear reality, and it may take a good deal of effort on our parts to take off our intellectual filters and face up to it forthrightly. But deep down we desperately want the real world instead of a pretend one, a real God instead of an abstract one, a God into whose mystery we can enter ever more profoundly rather than one who is only a conceptual problem to be analyzed from the outside. The virtual god worshiped by Eggheaders may stimulate the intellect, but its stark abstractness is ultimately too bleak. One can visit the Arctic but not live there.

Chapter 12

Letting God Be

To detach our desire from all good things and to wait. Experience proves that this waiting is satisfied. It is then that we touch the absolute good.

—SIMONE WEIL

Taking leave of God for the sake of God is the greatest act of renunciation that someone can make.

—MEISTER ECKHART[1]

Reading the novelist Nikos Kazantzakis can be a life-changing experience. Just one example of insightfulness is a scene from his *Zorba the Greek.*[2]

A man is walking on a heath on the isle of Crete. He's an intellectual—if he believed in God, he'd definitely be an

---

[1] Simone Weil, *Gravity and Grace* (London: Routledge and Kegan Paul, 1952), 13; Meister Eckhart, *Selected Writings,* ed. Brian Davies (New York: Penguin, 1994), 177.

[2] Nikos Kazantzakis, *Zorba the Greek* (New York: Simon and Schuster, 1952). Kazantzakis (1883–1957) was one of the most insightful novelists of the twentieth century. The film version of *Zorba the Greek*, directed by Michael Cacoyannis, appeared in 1964. The film is worth watching, but it is no replacement for the book.

Eggheader—so absorbed with bloodless abstractions and theories that he's generally uncomfortable in the messy world of actual objects, events, and persons. But on this particular day he finds himself enchanted by the physical landscape. The sun is pleasantly warm, summer insects are melodically chirping, the sky and ocean are a deep azure, and the shrubs that blanket the heath are fragrant. For the first time in years his senses are hungrily receptive to the world. He feels fully alive. He feels happy.

As he walks, he notices cocoons dangling from twigs on the aromatic shrubs. He pauses to take a closer look at one of them, and is startled and then delighted to see that the casing is aquiver. The butterfly inside is struggling to break free! Suddenly longing with all his being to serve as its midwife, the man snaps off the twig to which the cocoon is attached, cups it in his hands, raises it to his mouth, and gently exhales on it, hoping that the warmth of his breath will accelerate the butterfly's birth.

And it does. The cocoon's movements grow more agitated, and before long it breaks open. But to the man's horror, what emerges isn't the beautifully-winged creature he yearned to see, but a broken and wet monstrosity that feebly flaps its crumpled wings for a few seconds before collapsing in his hands. The man's eagerness to accelerate the birthing process forced the butterfly out before it was ready. It was untimely born and untimely died.

Impatience

Kazantzakis's parable is a chilling warning against impatiently rushing things. Not all things done hurriedly are done impatiently. Think of sprinting to catch a bus, responding to an emergency, or ice sculpting. But most of our kinetic and emotional running around is very much fueled by impatience. The culture in which we live actively encourages it. As one perceptive commentator notes:

We: Speed date. Eat fast food. Use the self-checkout lines in grocery stores. Try the "one weekend" diet. Pay extra for overnight shipping. Honk when the light turns green. Thrive or dive on quarterly earnings reports. Speak in half sentences. Start things but don't fin. . . . We twitter stories in 140 characters or less, yet some tweets are too long. We cut corners, take shortcuts. We txt.[3]

To be impatient is to be unwilling to wait. That much is obvious. The important question is why we find waiting so intolerable. The answer in most cases is anxiety and fear. We rush around because we're programmed by our fast-paced and success-oriented culture to fear wasting time or missing opportunities or losing control of the situation in which we find ourselves. We scamper because when we're anxious, we feel the need to be active, to take charge, to be productive, to get things, *anything,* done. Don't just sit there waiting! *Do* something! Be the master of your fate and the captain of your soul!

The fear or anxiety that breeds impatience oughtn't to be confused with prudence, although it sometimes is. Prudence tells us that it's reasonable to make a run for the bus when we have a good chance of catching it. Prudence tells the physician that her patient's appendix needs to come out *now,* and the ice sculptor that he can't dawdle too long over his block of ice. But while a prudent person knows that sometimes it's appropriate to do things in a hurry, she also knows that at other times the prudent thing is not to rush around at all but to bide her time, wait, look, think. Prudence is a child of reason and reflection, not panic. It's so essential when it comes to making wise decisions that the ancient philosophers considered it more than just a useful life skill. To them, it was a full-fledged virtue.

---

[3] Linton Weeks, "Impatient Nation: I Can't Wait for You to Read This," National Public Radio (December 6, 2010).

Fear, on the other hand, doesn't make rational appraisals of situations but urges immediate and usually unreflective fight or flight. A fearful person is impatient with prudent advice to consider alternative options or to wait and see. When a perceived threat arises, action needs to be taken—*now!* Moreover, impatience can become such a patterned response that it rears its head in situations where there's really no reason for anxiety or fear at all. Do we truly need to check email or Facebook every fifteen minutes? Is it going to kill us to wait in line for our morning latte? But just as anxiety and fear breed impatience, so impatience, when it becomes a habit, encourages us to react anxiously to everything. Because anxiety and impatience get slotted into the same psychological groove, one accompanies the other. So yes, we *do* need to check email endlessly because we get anxious if we don't and we don't like the experience of anxiety. Not getting instantly served by the *barista*? Ditto.

Chances are good that most of the things that make us anxious aren't worth getting excited about in the first place. But the habit of impatiently rushing around tends to make us tone deaf. So, like Katzantakis's character, we wind up doing foolish things that damage ourselves or others simply because we won't possess our souls in patience and wait.

This sounds pretty familiar, doesn't it? We've seen all along that fear is what drives idolatry. Now we have a better idea of why idolaters insist on rushing to grab onto gods who they think can both protect and instantly gratify them. Fear breeds impatience. Idolaters are too anxious to tolerate wandering in the desert in search of the "divine real deal," much less waiting for God to come to them. Why stand in line waiting for a cup of God? It's too risky.

But here's something else we've seen again and again: in their impatient unwillingness to wait for God until the time is ripe for God's emergence, idolaters violate just about every rule in the spiritual handbook. An authentic relationship with the living God can't be grounded in fear, and it certainly can't be rushed. In a real relationship with God, the worshiper knows better than to try to force God's hand or hurry God up. If the idols before whom we bow try to tell us otherwise, Eckhart's right. We really *ought* to pray God to be rid of them. We ought to renounce them. But renunciation is a bit trickier than it might appear.

The Greatest Renunciation

Although we humans seem to have a hardwired disposition for gluttony that makes us anxious about unmet desires and impatient to fulfill them, most of us, even Genieites in their better moments, recognize that indulging our every desire may not be especially good for us in the long run. So we periodically (especially at the beginning of a new year) try to cut back.

Sometimes our renunciations are motivated by concern for physical and emotional health. We reduce our intake of carbohydrates and fats and forego that extra hour of sleep to work out at the gym.

At other times renunciation is for the sake of moral well-being. All of us have secret guilty pleasures that may not harm others but that we suspect whittle away at our characters, if in no other way by adding a layer of moral flab to them. Sadly, many of us also indulge in some not-so-private guilty pleasures, ranging from rudeness to physical abuse, that hurt others. It's a rare person who hasn't taken the proverbial look in the mirror and resolved to do better.

Occasionally, we give up something just for the sake of testing our mettle. I once knew a man who smoked like a chimney. I've never known a heavier tobacco user. But three or four times a year he'd put away his cigarettes and pipes for a solid two weeks. He had no intention of quitting the habit, even though he knew all its health risks. His goal was to assert his autonomy over tobacco. If he continued to smoke, it was because he chose to, not because he was enslaved by the drug. (I make no comment on whether this was all a rather elaborate exercise in self-deception.)

Unhappy experience testifies to the likelihood that many of our renunciations, regardless of how earnestly we make them, ultimately fail to stick. New Year's resolutions deflate in February, expensive exercise equipment gathers dust, and the porn filter on the computer is guiltily switched off. Adding insult to injury, good-intentioned renunciations sometimes pave the road to hell, because once we fall back into the habits we tried to break, we can do so with abandoned gusto, apparently embracing an "in for a penny, in for a pound" philosophy. Perhaps this is the meaning behind the New Testament's observation that if a badly exorcised demon returns to its victim, it brings along lots of its pals.

When our renunciations go sour, one common response is to chalk our failure up to "biting off more than we could chew." Next time, we resolve, we'll be a bit more realistic, we'll pace ourselves, we won't start off by jumping into the deep end. But the truth of the matter is that we fail precisely because we *don't* dive straight into the depths. We're too timid in exorcising the demons we want to get rid of. And the explanation for our timidity isn't hard to come by. We're not very good at renouncing for the same reason we're not good at waiting patiently: fear. We're frightened of making the commitment and taking the plunge necessary to truly wean ourselves off bad habits. That would involve venturing too far away from our comfort zones. So we renounce a little bit and we wait a little bit, and when the initial resolution wears thin, we slide back to where we started.

If we really want to get somewhere, we need to dive deep. Happily, we're not totally on our own, because spiritual masters from all traditions are remarkably unanimous in their descriptions of the different levels of renunciation necessary for liberation. They tell us that if we merely try to renounce unwanted behavior such as overeating, under-exercising, or rudeness, we're only dabbling our toes in the water. To get serious, we need to touch base with and expunge the underlying desires that motivate unwanted behavior in the first place. Swearing off a specific pattern of behavior without doing something about its source is like chopping down a weed at ground level but neglecting to yank up its roots.

Once we become mindful of the desires that behaviorally pull us hither and yon, we also realize that they all lead back to what philosopher and novelist Iris Murdoch calls the "fat relentless ego," which impatiently (not to mention incessantly) clamors to be fed, protected, and praised, and plaintively whimpers or throws tantrums when it isn't.[4] It's the ego that confuses license with freedom, demands instant gratification, is always anxious, and restlessly searches for idols—which are nothing but idealized projections of the ego—that it hopes will offer protection. So if we truly want to do something about the desires that motivate unwanted behavior as well as the urge toward idolatry, it's necessary to discipline the ego.

This process can be painful. It requires that we strip away the noisy ego layer by layer, progressively shedding the complex network of behavioral patterns, cravings, secret fears, and personality traits by which we typically define ourselves. This network is what Thomas Merton and others call the "false self," and once we manage to rid ourselves of it, spiritual masters assure us, we're well and truly liberated and finally able to open up to the world as it is and, more important, to God. The egoistic blinkers born of fear and desire finally come off. We've made the Greatest Renunciation.[5]

This is the usual story, and it's true enough so far as it goes. But Meister Eckhart believes it's incomplete. Shedding ego *isn't* the greatest renunciation. If we wish to be genuinely free of enslavement to our fears and desires and the idols they

---

[4] Iris Murdoch, *Existentialists and Mystics* (New York: Penguin, 1997), 342.

[5] For a lengthy discussion of the distinction between true and false self, see Kerry Walters, *Soul Wilderness: A Desert Spirituality* (Mahwah, NJ: Paulist Press, 2001).

spawn, if we hope to authentically open ourselves to the living God, we must stretch for one more level of renunciation. The sheer audacity of what Eckhart says is enough to induce spiritual vertigo:

> Taking leave of God for the sake of God is the greatest act of renunciation that someone can make. Now St. Paul renounced God for the sake of God: he left all that he could get from God and he left all that God could give him and all that he could receive from God. When he took leave of these things, he renounced God for the sake of God, and yet God remained with him, as God exists in himself, not according to the manner in which he is gained or received but according to the being that he himself is.[6]

We need to be careful here not to water down Eckhart's message to make it more palatable. The most comfortable interpretation is that he's urging us to throw over our idols. If we lowercase some of his references to God in this passage, just as we did in Chapter 1 when taking a look at his claim that we ought to ask God to rid us of god, we can arrive at this conclusion easily enough. We need to take leave of god for God. Saint Paul renounced god for the sake of God. And so on.

I don't think this way of reading the passage is totally misguided. It only stands to reason, given the fact that the idols we venerate are idealized self-projections, that when we discipline our egos, our idols are exposed for the false gods they are. But if this is all that Eckhart means, it's surprising that he would describe the renunciation as the greatest one we can make. The magnitude of a renunciation, after all, is proportionate to the draw or desirability of whatever's renounced. No matter how attached we are to our idols, forsaking them can't be the greatest thing we could renounce. They just don't have that much juice.

---

[6] Eckhart, *Selected Writings*, 177.

So Eckhart must have another kind of renunciation in mind, and to grasp it we need to take his uppercase references to God seriously. Once our false images of God have been repudiated, once we've managed to get past the egoistic flaws, fears, and desires that constructed the idols in the first place, we have one more renunciation, the greatest of them all, to make. We have to give up *God—for the sake of God.* This isn't just a bewildering thing to say. It's also a sword through the heart. It's painful enough to give up a mortal beloved. It's excruciating beyond words to give up The Beloved. And yet, says Eckhart, we must.

This, then, is the Greatest Renunciation. But whatever does it mean?

Divine No-thingness

Eckhart's getting at something like this. Not even our most "orthodox," nonidolatrous ways of thinking and talking about God capture the divine essence, as God truly is. They inevitably leave us with an incomplete and distorted notion of God. So the God we worship is God as "gained or received" by us. Not even our most traditional and hallowed utterances about God—"God is love," for example, or "Jesus is the Way, the Truth, and the Light"—stretch to God "as he exists in himself." It's not that they're false, exactly. But at best, they can only hint at the true nature of God. So if we want to honor God as God truly exists, we ought to give them up.

What would happen if we acknowledged, seriously and not just for the sake of argument, that our endless talk about God—our theological analyses, our liturgical rituals, our worded prayers and petitions, our private devotions—says everything about God as God is gained or received by us, but leaves untouched God as God truly exists? How would such an admission affect us and our relationship to God? In making the Greatest Renunciation recommended by Eckhart, would we lose everything? And if so, what would be the point?

Our initial response to the Greatest Renunciation might well be a bone-chilling sense of nothingness, of void, of a cosmic emptiness that leaves us cowering in the dark like lost children. But before we utterly despair, we ought to consider this: There's nothing, and then there's nothing. Sometimes nothingness reveals itself as complete desolation with no future, no way out, no hope. Remember the parable of the Prodigal Son? We're told that after taking his dad's money, he traveled to a distant land where he met with such disaster that he fell into hopelessness. The Greek that's translated "distant land" is actually *khora makra,* "the big emptiness." It's the kind of nothingness that kills body and soul.

But there's also the nothing that nurtures rather than kills. The word *khora* can also mean "womb," and it's in this sense that the Greatest Renunciation reveals something essential although also incomprehensible about God. God as God truly exists is the great No-thingness unlimited by space and time (things, after all, are defined by precisely such limitations), the divine No-thingness that is absolute vitality, pure fecundity, undiminishing activity. The divine No-thingness is the loving womb that births and sustains everything that is, and it is the polar opposite of the dreadful *khora makra* that all of us rightfully fear. But we simply can't know it or speak it adequately. Because language is most comfortable when describing things, our attempts to say something about God are liable to wind up reducing God to the status of just another thing. So instead of straining to peg down the divine No-thingness with more and more chatter (I think here of Lilliputians futilely scurrying to tie Gulliver down to the ground), perhaps we'd be better off embracing an *unspeaking* of the divine No-thingness that frees us of limiting and distorting words and opens us up to the possibility of experiencing the deep silence in which dwells God as God truly exists.

When we realize that the Greatest Renunciation puts us in touch with the life-generating No-thingness rather than a dead big emptiness, our initial forlornness is replaced with a fulfilled sense of homecoming. Divine No-thingness meets us, speaks to us in the language of silence, and in doing so paradoxically reveals itself as pure Presence, womb love. Gabriel Marcel, as we saw in Chapter 11, calls this the experience of mystery. Eckhart, himself struggling for adequate words, calls it "a single oneness" or "pure union." There's no longer a need for God as gained and received by us, much less a need for idols, because we have been touched by a present No-thingness that needs no words. Indescribable as it is, however, the meeting so completes us that we become, as Eckhart says, "truly human." We become what we were made to be.[7]

We shouldn't imagine that this silent experience of the divine No-thingness invalidates liturgy, theology, poetry, the musical and visual arts, or any other medium in which we struggle to say something about God. The experience of God's essential mysteriousness will always induce in us an overflow of awe and love that strives for ways to express itself, and our lives are richer for it. But the mystery helps us keep perspective. We realize that all our efforts to speak the divine No-thingness forever fall short of the mark, however beautifully evocative they may be. This inclines us away from mistaking God as gained and received by us from God as God truly exists, but even more from the crude temptation of idolatry. When compared to the genuine experience of God made possible by the Greatest Renunciation, the otherwise attractive concreteness of idols is not so much unappealing as lifelessly boring.

If the silent sinking into the divine No-thingness recommended by Eckhart sounds like mysticism, that's because it is. But *mysticism* too often carries esoteric and arcane connotations. Mystics, we conventionally think, are those special individuals who are heads and shoulders above the rest of us when it comes to spiritual sensitivity. Only a tiny handful of people in each generation, we believe, are capable of such attunement. But Eckhart is dubious about this claim, and so am I. The Greatest Renunciation is open to all. Everyone, not just

---

[7] Ibid.

a few pure souls, has the potential to be a mystic. Otherwise, only a handful of us could ever become "truly human," as Eckhart says, and this sort of arbitrary favoritism is unthinkable in a loving God.

Nor should we jump to the conclusion that thinking of God as divine No-thingness contradicts the rich concreteness of the God portrayed in scripture. It's true that the Old Testament often offers anthropomorphized descriptions of God and that the New Testament robustly proclaims that Jesus is God incarnate. But we mustn't overlook, even though we frequently do if we become too focused on God as gained and received by us, that the unfathomably mysterious nature of God remains a steady theme throughout the entire Bible. Exodus describes God as enshrouded in a "thick darkness" or impenetrable "cloud" (20:21; 24:15). Job ultimately bows his head and submits to the impossibility of understanding God or God's ways (42:2–3). The Psalmist says that "such knowledge [of God] is too wonderful for me; it is so high that I cannot attain it" (139:6). And the prophet Isaiah, in denouncing the foolishness of idolatry, reminds us that God is "a God who hides himself" (45:15). The Hebrew word translated "hides" means "to be absent," "to conceal," or "to keep secret." Isaiah knew that God is the divine No-thingness.

New Testament authors likewise acknowledge that even Jesus, God's most concrete revelation, remains shrouded in mystery despite his embodiment—or more accurately *because* of it. His very existence baffles even the apostles, his closest day-to-day companions, who constantly misunderstood who he was. John, the beloved disciple whom tradition tells us was closer to Jesus than any of his other followers, came to the conclusion that the full truth about Jesus is unknowable to the world (14:17). Jesus is the Light that illuminates the world. But Light stared at directly blinds. The entire Prologue of the Gospel According to John, in fact, may be read as a beautifully poetic stab at staring into the Light's dark brilliance. In a similar way Paul describes God as both kind and severe (Rom 11:22), his gifts "indescribable" (2 Cor 9:15), and his peace as surpassing "all understanding" (Phil 4:7). The Incarnation gives us brief glimpses of what God is, but at the same time it also only deepens the mystery. The very act of divine self-emptying underscores God's elusive hiddenness (Phil 2:5–7), just as a lit match temporarily provides just enough illumination to make us aware of how much dark surrounds us. John, speaking for himself and everyone else who knew Jesus, expresses the inexhaustible incomprehensibility of the God-man when he touchingly concludes his Gospel with the confession that the world itself couldn't possibly hold all the books that could be written about Jesus (21:25). Thousands and millions and billions of words, and still the physical incarnation of God, who you'd think would clear up all the mystery once and for all, remains a cipher. Yet—and perhaps this is the greatest mystery of all—the cipher lovingly invites us to enter ever more deeply into the Greatest Renunciation so that we may become fully human. And we respond.

For elusive though the revelation of God in Christ remains, Christ's life, teaching, sacrifice, and resurrection *do* tell us something profound about the living God: whatever else God is, God is preeminently love. The divine *Khora* loves creation into existence and sustains its being, tenderly and vigilantly keeping watch over it as a hen broods over her chicks. Whenever we come into genuine contact with the loving divine Presence, we are suffused with the realization that all is ultimately well, even if life isn't terribly pleasant at the moment.

Love, after all, oughtn't to be confused with mere feeling, on the one hand, or a ceaseless bestowal of everything asked for, on the other. The first is sentimentality; the second is the demand of a spoiled child—or adult idolater. Instead, genuine love is the desire for the beloved's well-being without expectation of anything in return, a heartfelt wish to serve the beloved so that that person's life is enriched, broadened, and deepened. It is a freely bestowed gift, and like all gifts, love is given not as reward or incentive but simply out of overflowing good will. When you and I love appropriately, we stretch our typically self-centered natures to act benevolently for the

beloved's sake. But God doesn't merely possess the poten-
tiality for loving. God *is* love, and whenever we experience
love, whether offered by God or a fellow human, we sense a
hint of the Divine on the wind. The face of love can take on
many forms, but behind each of them shimmers the presence
of God. Yet under normal circumstances, it's the face, not the
divine love that animates it, that we notice most immediately.
The divine presence behind the face never comes as sharply
into focus. And yet those of us who have experienced it know
beyond a shadow of a doubt that it's there.

A perfectly reasonable question at this point: Why are we
typically allowed but a hint of the Divine? Why must it be
this way? We're happy to give up idols, because we've seen
again and again that the worship of them is destructive. But
why must the living God remain so elusive, even when he
incarnates as Jesus the Christ?

The simple answer, of course, is that *God is God* and so
must forever defy our limited thing-oriented intellects and
imaginations. How can mere sponges possibly hope to absorb the ocean? Pile up all the words that the world has ever
known, and they still won't utter divine No-thingness.

Another answer is that God, who is love through and
through, is apprehended in direct proportion to how well we
love in turn. In loving us into being and sustaining us, God
reveals as much of God's true self as possible. But even that
comparatively infinitesimal revelation is ungraspable if we
fail to open ourselves up in love to receive it. In other words,
God's elusiveness is largely because of God's nature, but also
because we blind ourselves by our adherence to idols.

There's an additional explanation for divine elusiveness,
and it goes back to the distinction between freedom-from and
freedom-to explored in Chapter 1. We saw there that even
though idolaters think of freedom solely in terms of liberation
from objects of fear, genuine freedom also requires the ability
and willingness on our part to venture beyond comfort zones
toward new possibilities. Exercising freedom-to is inevitably

risky because it takes us to undiscovered lands. But in its absence, we fail to thrive. We become Miss Havishams, locked
up in the present because we're too frightened to step into the
future. So we settle for dead idols, in whom there is no risk
because there's no mystery.

But the living God, the great *Khora* who lovingly births and
nurtures us and desires our spiritual development, chooses to
remain just out of reach, an elusive presence, an experienced
but ungraspable No-thingness, to entice us away from our
safe idols into the risky but ultimately rewarding business of
giving ourselves up to love. Stepping out of our snug temples
into the open air can be frightening, but it's also exhilarat-
ing, and once we breathe it in it's unlikely that we'll return
to our musty idols or even to God as gained and received by
us. In refusing to be as palpably concrete as an idol, God isn't
playing a game of cat-and-mouse with us. He withdraws so
that we may exercise the *freedom to* follow and, in following, to thrive.

Letting-Be

A key word for Eckhart, *gelassenheit,* often translated as
"detachment," refers to the spiritual practice of liberating ourselves from both idols and the less soul-enslaving assumption
that the gained and received God is identical to God as God
truly exists. But I think Eckhart's meaning is more accurately
captured if we render *gelassenheit* as "letting-be." Letting-be
mustn't be confused with a passive sitting on one's hands or
a timid withdrawal from an unpleasant situation, as when
we plead, "Just let me be!" On the contrary, letting-be is an
intensely alert attentiveness to reality that seeks to experience
rather than to manipulate. It is a profound receptivity, and it's
our natural state when our spirits aren't cluttered with desire
or fear. It's not only a necessary condition for accurately reading the world around us. It's also an essential discipline for
making the Greatest Renunciation. The anonymous author

of the fourteenth-century mystical text *The Cloud of Unknowing* called it a "naked intent" to open oneself to divine No-thingness.[8] Twentieth-century French mystic Simone Weil, who well knew that "contact with God is given us through the sense of absence," called it "waiting for God."[9] T. S. Eliot hauntingly expressed the same insight:

> I said to my soul be still, and let the darkness
> > come upon you
> Which shall be the darkness of God.[10]

When you and I cultivate the spirit of letting-be, we permit both God and ourselves to be who we are. Eckhart said that when we embrace the Greatest Renunciation, we give up God *for the sake of God.* His meaning is deliberately double edged. On the one hand, the Greatest Renunciation is undertaken by us *for the sake of* a meeting with divine No-thingness that will complete us. Letting God be who God is rather than trying to corral God with our words, detaching ourselves from the gained and received God to whom we so often cling, is for our own good. But at the same time, because letting God be refuses to impose a false identity upon God, we also honor God. We bow before God's mystery, acknowledging its irreducibility and opening ourselves to it in anticipation of a revelation. We restrain our impatience, refusing to rush God in the way that Kazantzakis's character rushed the butterfly. We wait. We give up God *for God's sake.* We let God be.

To an idolater, all this is bewildering and perhaps annoying nonsense. For him, the only god worthy of his attention is one that's concretely present and ready to serve. He wouldn't dream of waiting for *his* god. Instead, he impatiently expects

---

[8] *The Cloud of Unknowing* is a mystical text written in Middle English sometime in the latter half of the fourteenth century.

[9] Simone Weil, *The Notebooks of Simone Weil*, 2 vols. (London: Routledge and Kegan Paul, 1956), 1:239.

[10] T. S. Eliot, *Four Quartets* (New York: Harvest Books, 1943). The passage is from "East Coker," the second quartet.

his god to wait for *him*. It's an audacious but not surprising reversal of roles, because we already know that the idolater's ultimate concern is himself rather than God. His world is so filled with himself, his fears, and his desires, that there's simply no room left over for anything else, even divine No-thingness.

But here's the good news, attested to by Eckhart and countless others. Although idolaters can come across as intractably enslaved by the fears that bind them to their false gods, none is beyond redemption. The God who created us, as Augustine said, also made us yearn for God. So no matter how deeply we fall into idolatry or how often we backslide into the worship of false gods—and most of us will do so from time to time, especially during spells of crisis—*Khora* beckons, divine No-thingness ceaselessly and patiently invites us forth. No idol can do that.